Better Homes and Gardens®

celebrate the SEASON® 2008

Meredith® Books
Des Moines, Iowa

Better Homes and Gardens®

Celebrate the Season® 2008

Editor: Lois White
Contributing Editor and Project Designer: Susan Banker
Contributing Food Editors: Winifred Moranville,
    Joyce Trollope
Contributing Art Director/Graphic Designer: Catherine Brett
Copy Chief: Doug Kouma
Copy Editor: Kevin Cox
Publishing Operations Manager: Karen Schirm
Edit and Design Production Coordinator: Mary Lee Gavin
Editorial Assistant: Sheri Cord
Book Production Managers: Marjorie J. Schenkelberg,
    Mark Weaver
Contributing Copy Editor: M. Peg Smith
Contributing Proofreaders: Judy Friedman, Karen Grossman,
    Gretchen Kauffman
Contributing Photographers: Marty Baldwin, Jason Donnelly,
    Scott Little, Blaine Moats, Jason Wilde
Contributing Technical Illustrator: Chris Neubauer
    Graphics, Inc.
Contributing Project Designers: Margaret Sindelar, Rachel
    Sindelar, Alice Wetzel, Emma Wetzel
Contributing Recipe Developers: Ellen Boeke,
    Mittie Hellmich
Test Kitchen Director: Lynn Blanchard
Test Kitchen Product Supervisor: Jill Moberly
Test Kitchen Culinary Specialists: Marilyn Cornelius, Juliana
    Hale, Maryellyn Krantz, Colleen Weeden, Lori Wilson
Test Kitchen Nutrition Specialists: Elizabeth Burt, R.D.,
    L.D.; Laura Marzen, R.D., L.D.

Meredith® Books
Editorial Director: John Riha
Deputy Editor: Jennifer Darling
Managing Editor: Kathleen Armentrout
Brand Manager: Janell Pittman
Group Editor: Jan Miller
Senior Associate Design Director: Mick Schnepf

Director, Marketing and Publicity: Amy Nichols
Executive Director, Sales: Ken Zagor
Director, Operations: George A. Susral
Director, Production: Douglas M. Johnston
Business Director: Janice Croat

Vice President and General Manager, SIM: Jeff Myers

Better Homes and Gardens® **Magazine**
Editor in Chief: Gayle Goodson Butler
Senior Deputy Editor, Home Design: Oma Blaise Ford
Deputy Editor, Food and Entertaining: Nancy Wall Hopkins

Meredith Publishing Group
President: Jack Griffin
President, *Better Homes and Gardens*®: Andy Sareyan
Vice President, Corporate Solutions: Michael Brownstein
Vice President, Manufacturing: Bruce Heston
Vice President, Consumer Marketing: David Ball
Director, Creative Services: Grover Kirkman
Consumer Product Marketing Director: Steve Swanson
Consumer Product Marketing Manager: Wendy Merical
Business Director: Jim Leonard

Meredith Corporation
Chairman of the Board: William T. Kerr
President and Chief Executive Officer: Stephen M. Lacy

In Memoriam: E.T. Meredith III (1933–2003)

Our seal assures you that every recipe in
Celebrate the Season 2008 has been tested in
the Better Homes and Gardens® Test Kitchen.
This means that each recipe is practical and
reliable, and meets our high standards of taste
appeal. We guarantee your satisfaction with
this book for as long as you own it.

table *of* contents

setting the stage

Embrace year-end seasons with glorious, easy-to-do decorations. From crisp, colorful autumn to merry days leading to Christmas, your home will shine with festive creativity.

gathering together

Make memories bright for everyone who visits. Serve delectable meals, set a magical atmosphere, and plan surprises so spectacular that ol' St. Nick himself would be delighted.

3

giving from the heart

Roll and dip candies, stitch a pillow cover, stir and toast a snack mix, or cover an album. From your home and hands, these gifts are filled with love.

just for kids

Gather little ones to play with pasta, tear tissue paper, or express themselves with paint. These fun projects will keep them busy. Be sure to have lots of supplies on hand; they may want to make one for you!

In a Twinkling
Easy projects you can make in an evening's time.

Surprises

sprinkle the holiday season with magic. A favorite memory for me is the year that tiny gifts perched among branches of our family's tree. My brothers and I assumed the pretty packages, wrapped in embossed silver paper and tied with generous red satin ribbons, were Dad's gifts to Mom. Detectives that we were, we concluded they were jewelry, each piece wrapped separately.

Then on Christmas Eve, Mom handed each of us one of the elegantly wrapped gifts. My ring box held a spool of bright red thread. In boxes for each of my brothers were fishing line and a ball of yarn. Then Mom told us to close our eyes. When we opened them, she had unrolled our various strings and instructed us to follow our lines to find our gifts. We laughed with frenzy as we untangled our fibers from doorknobs, lampshades, and each other.

At the tail of my thread was a brand-new cabinet-style sewing machine. At 16, I suddenly felt so grown up. I had graduated from dolls, puzzles, and board games to something I'd use and treasure for years.

This sweet memory came back to me as I was making the tiny boxes shown on the cover and **pages 142–143**. My friend's little girl, Rosie, was fascinated by the mini treasures, as if each one held its own bit of magic. She smiled as she discovered small candies and notes that she promptly asked her mom to read. One message, "Sleep by the Christmas tree," stayed in her darling little head, and that's just where she ended up that night.

Within the pages of this book, I hope you'll discover fun ways to surprise the special people in your life. Maybe it will be a new Christmas Eve recipe, a fresh decorating scheme, or an idea for a gift that's just perfect. Wherever you find the magic, here's wishing you and yours the season's best hidden treasures.

Merry surprises,

Sue Banker

Sue Banker

6

See "Pretty as a Postcard", page 32.

SETTING the STAGE

Bring on the joy of the season. Decorate to celebrate every day from Thanksgiving to that magical day the jolly ol' soul arrives. Discover easy yet artful touches to fill your home with warmth and wonder.

7

the fibers of fall

Woven, tied, stitched, or wrapped, ribbons and fabrics in autumn hues bring the glorious colors of the season to life on tables and walls.

8

autumn-weave table mat

〰 Natural burlap is a rugged background for weaving ribbons and fibers of orange, yellow, purple, red, brown, and green.

1 Cut a circle from burlap. Remove approximately 1 inch of thread from edge to fringe.

2 Pull groups of cross threads to make space to weave in ribbons and fibers.

3 Weave in ribbons and fibers, using a needle if desired. Weave over and under randomly or in a pattern, such as repeating over five and under two.

4 Trim ribbon and fiber ends even with burlap edges.

felted leaf table runner

〰 Pretty plaid wool is layered with autumn designs. Leaves are tacked in place using a simple felting process, making the detailed table runner a fun project that can be completed in only an evening.

1 Trace leaf patterns, **page 154**. Use the patterns to cut leaves from wool fabric.

2 Following directions on the needle felting tool and mat package, felt leaf shapes onto the table runner.

3 Using felting tool, add veins to leaves with novelty yarn.

4 Embellish leaves by sewing buttons at stem ends.

10

What You'll Need...

- two 18-inch-diameter wire floral wreath forms

- scissors

- 1½-inch-wide bias-cut silk ribbon to wrap around wreath form

- sewing needle and heavyweight thread

- 3 yards of sheer wire-edge ribbon for bow

- crafts wire

- ruler

- approximately 100 yards of ¾- to 1½-inch-wide ribbon or bias-cut fabric strips

- copper leaf-shape cookie cutter

A band of natural raffia makes this candle special. To give a focal point, knot several strands of red-dyed raffia around the band. Nestle the earthy candle in a wood pedestal dish filled with putkas (pods available with potpourri supplies) in all the season's best colors. **Note:** Never leave burning candles unattended.

raffia-wrapped candle

blaze of color wreath

Gather an abundance of ribbon and fabric in autumn hues to make a nature-inspired wreath.

1 For wreath back, wrap one floral form with bias-cut silk ribbon. Secure ends together with needle and thread.

2 Make a large bow with wire-edge ribbon. Secure with crafts wire. Set aside the bow.

3 Cut remaining ribbon and fabric in 9-inch lengths, cutting diagonally to add dimension to the wreath.

4 Attach ribbons randomly to the unwrapped wire wreath form using an overhand loop and filling spaces to create fullness.

5 Using needle and two strands of strong thread, sew the two wreaths together back to back.

6 Attach bow, cookie cutter, and hanging loop with crafts wire.

simple thanks

With plenty of hustle and bustle in the kitchen, you can relax knowing the Thanksgiving table is gorgeous. With only a few minutes and a little help from Mother Nature, you can achieve this elegant setting.

pretty places

Drape a coordinating-color fabric napkin across stacked dishes to dress place settings. Top with a personalized pumpkin, tuck napkin ends under the plate, and set the stack on a woven mat. Add natural touches with snips of bittersweet and wheat.

ahhh, natural

❧ Tone on tone is key to the success of this attractive center-of-the-table arrangement. Cream-color ceramic pieces play off the pumpkins' uniformity. Mix in a few gourds and branches of bittersweet, and food will vie for attention at your table.

perfect-pick chair backs

❧ To perk up a chair back, place a burlap square on point. Tuck five wheat stalks into the weave of the burlap, making a graphic statement.

personalized to the letter

❧ Creamy enamel paint is perfect to add initials to pint-size pumpkins. No need for patterns—informal hand-lettering gives the accents charm.

autumnal
wonders

Savor the beauty of autumn with projects reminiscent of the outdoors. Combine pinecones, cloved oranges, kumquats, and more in fresh-scented arrangements.

bountiful baskets

∿ Seasonal selections turn a trio of baskets into a hearty stacked display. Center and stack baskets, using floral foam to secure. Arrange clove-studded oranges, kumquats, pinecones, evergreen branches, and seeded eucalyptus among the baskets. Top with a candle for a touch of light. **Note:** Never leave burning candles unattended.

striking centerpiece

∿ Bright and bold, this eye-pleasing centerpiece grabs attention. Fill a glass hurricane container with kumquats, top with a pinecone-shape candle, and tuck in a few evergreen sprigs. Tie a silky bow around the container, leaving one ribbon tail gracefully longer.

17

bright on white

Add magic to the table with a white feather tree. Natural additions—ornaments of dried orange slices, kumquats, and pinecones—allow the simplicity of the tree to shine.

blooming harvest

Combine backyard finds with fruit, spices, and natural accents in a bountiful fall display. Large pinecones, clove-studded oranges, clusters of juicy kumquats, seeded eucalyptus, and wheat sprays brim from a sturdy basket. Roses, fresh from a florist and in tiny vials of water, soften the overall appearance.

What You'll Need...

- white spruce pinecones from 1 to 2 inches long
- kumquats
- wire wreath form
- hot-glue gun and glue sticks
- wide ribbon

fruitful season

〜 Add spicy citrus fragrance to your home with clove-studded clementines nestled in a bowl of glossy red cranberries.

spruced-up wreath

〜 A simply chic wreath of orderly white spruce pinecones and kumquats adds a graphic flourish to the mantel or door.

1 Sort the pinecones and kumquats by size, from largest to smallest.

2 Glue horizontal rows of pinecones and kumquats to the wreath with the largest pinecones and kumquats on the outer edge and using gradually smaller pinecones and kumquats toward the center.

3 Tie a ribbon bow and attach it with glue at the top of the wreath.

▶ **Bountiful Basket** An arrangement of gourds, silk flowers, acorns, and colorful feathers will be a hit all autumn. Select a wrought-iron basket and use crafts wire and heavy-duty glue dots (available where gift basket supplies are sold) to assemble the arrangement. To wire gourds to the basket, first poke starter holes with an ice pick or the end of a large paper clip.

In a Twinkling
fall into it

◀ **It All Stacks Up** Wooden trunks, crates, drawers, and ladders have interesting nooks and crannies to display pumpkins and gourds. Add texture and design to the spaces with fabric napkins, place mats, and ribbon in rustic plaids and stripes.

Just Plain Gourdeous Saw off the end of a clean dried gourd to make a wall vase that holds autumn's bounty. Drill two small holes approximately 1½ inches apart on the back; thread with wire to hang. Leave the gourd natural or spray it with stain. Tie a ribbon bow around the narrow portion and fill with dried flowers.

Sign of the Times A leaf rake propped against a tree trunk is a handsome yard accent. Wrap the rake handle with ribbon and hot-glue silk leaves near the bottom to resemble just-swept leaves. Add pumpkins, raffia, and a bittersweet vine to complete the harvest setting.

Picture Perfect Back a weathered frame with chicken wire as the canvas for colorful finds. Glue or wire real or silk leaves, bittersweet vines, berries, and cattails to the wire or frame.

make it sparkle

Candlelight—amid metallics and clear, frosted, and cut glass—warms the scene richly. Assemble these arrangements in minutes before guests come a-caroling.

silver and gold

A medley of glassware becomes a set as it rises on top of a sparkling clear cake stand. Filled with metal-encased tea lights and surrounded with a sprinkling of gold-tone decorator stones, the arrangement glows brilliantly. To multiply the sparkles, set the cake stand on a mirrored place mat. **Note:** Never leave burning candles unattended.

eclectic sensation

Silver-leaf pomegranates make a dazzling display in glass containers with silver beads. A purchased faux crystal and silver button wreath surrounds the gathering. To make silvery pomegranates, brush fruits with sizing adhesive according to manufacturer's directions. Apply sheets of silver leaf, then burnish with a clean, dry art brush.

the collector's Christmas

By intention or chance, accumulating holiday decorations is natural. When grouped, they make stunning collections that focus on color, design, or theme.

top it off

The Christmas tree needs only one, so show off the remainder of your tree toppers on a tabletop. This easy-to-make holder has stationary dowels for precious glass trophies to stand safely.

1 For each tree topper, place a dowel in a wooden ball, pressing it in as far as it reaches but not through to the other side.

2 Carefully place a topper on each dowel to determine how long each dowel needs to be, allowing each topper to rest on the ball. With a pencil, mark where to cut the dowel.

3 Use a handsaw to cut the dowels where marked.

4 Place toppers on dowels and arrange them on the flat rim of the plate, spacing evenly. Mark placement with a pencil.

5 Use wood glue to adhere balls and dowels on the plate. Let glue dry.

6 In a well-ventilated work area, spray-paint the topper holder gold. Let paint dry.

7 Arrange toppers as planned. Tuck greenery among toppers and place small ornaments and a bow.

What You'll Need ...

- ⅜-inch wooden dowels
- wooden balls with ⅜-inch holes
- collection of tree topper ornaments
- pencil
- handsaw
- large wooden plate with flat rim
- wood glue
- gold spray paint
- greenery
- small ornaments
- ribbon

27

Creative Collections

Consider a multitude of holiday displays, drawing inspiration from these themes.

reindeer
prance them along the center of a dining table on a bright red runner

snowflakes
dangle from fish line in a window or from a chandelier

polar animals, such as polar bears and penguins
prop on a sled surrounded by artificial snow

nutcrackers
intersperse with greenery in a wicker basket

Christmas card photos
tie to a fresh green wreath with curling ribbon

angels
group them with musical instruments on holiday sheet music

cookie cutters
place them in an extra-large clear glass cookie jar topped with a generous ribbon bow

merry flock

If you collect ornaments of a particular theme, let your imagination soar beyond evergreen branches. The iron cage is a perfect nest for a menagerie of glass birds. Cages often can be found in antiques, crafts, pet, and home decor stores. A sprinkling of flocked greenery and battery-operated mini lights complete the radiant arrangement of feathered friends.

jeweled trees

Spray a grapevine wreath with a dusting of gold paint to back a collection of holiday pins. This presentation can stay the same or expand. Stop at a small collection, placed closely together, or keep adding to it for years until the wreath is filled. To create interest in open spaces, tuck in artificial berries and gold leaves.

punch bowl souls

Vintage Santas fill a wonderfully tarnished punch bowl to the brim. The old fellows and the worn patina of the silver pieces complement each other perfectly.

snow much fun

Old and new, big and small—snowfolks of all sorts are assembled in an oh-so-friendly neighborhood. Perched on shelves, the cold-weather characters are unified amid snowflakes and miniature evergreens. Place a few snowmen in clear glass containers with acrylic "ice" nuggets. With so many smiles in a group, the jolly mood is sure to be contagious.

pretty as a postcard

Vintage postcards, with scenes of days gone by, are inexpensive art pieces to use in holiday decorating. Many colorful cards are sold in antiques stores and usually cost less than new greeting cards.

tabletop classics

∾ All eyes will feast on the cheerful artwork, hand-written messages, and dated postage stamps around a table layered with vintage holiday greetings. The postcard-size art, when photocopied and enlarged, also wraps around centerpiece packages and little party favors.

personally yours

∾ Address each guest's place setting with a pair of postcards sandwiched between red and clear glass plates. To continue the theme, craft a postmark napkin ring from a postcard strip wrapped around a plain ring. Be sure to make photocopies, preserving the original postcards.

suited for framing

A framed postcard, set on a tabletop or hung on a wall, places holiday decor at eye level. To back the pretty picture, align a pair of coordinating papers and cover the seam with a short length of ribbon. Complete the picture with precut mats and frames, available in crafts and discount stores.

34

picturesque pillow

Perk up a pillow with a favorite wintry postcard scene. With all of the copy-and-iron transfers available today, this easy-sew pillow is a breeze to make.

NOTE For sewing, use ½-inch seams. Stitch right sides facing unless otherwise instructed.

1 Enlarge design to 10×14 inches and transfer postcard design to transfer paper at a professional copy center.

2 Following transfer manufacturer's directions, transfer design to fabric, allowing at least ½ inch on all sides. Trim away excess fabric, keeping design evenly centered while maintaining the ½ inch for seam allowances.

3 Cut 4 wool sashings 3½ inches wide. Stitch to bottom and top edges first, then to sides. Cut pillow back the same size as the front.

4 Sew pillow front to pillow back, right sides together, leaving an opening to insert pillow form.

5 Turn right side out. Insert pillow form. Topstitch ¾ inch from outer edge to create flange. Using gold metallic topstitching thread, decorative-stitch along flange, zigzagging over two strands of gold metallic pearl cotton.

6 Hand-stitch opening closed. Stitch 3 jingle bells to each corner of the design.

postcard ornaments

Hang postcards on tree branches. To make ornaments quickly, punch a hole at the top and thread narrow ribbon through the hole. Tie the ends in a bow, making a loop for hanging. To leave a valuable postcard intact, make color photocopies or back it with cardstock, trim ½ inch larger, and thread ribbon through a hole punched in the backing.

attention to detail

Supersize graphic postcards with a 300 percent color enlargement. The large scale really shows off beautiful detail, including the year on the postmark. Back enlargements with slightly larger thin boards painted red. Drill two holes through the center of the back board and thread with wire for hanging. Hot-glue layers together, top with greenery and a bow, and this magnified postcard duo is ready to hang.

garlands all around

String a plethora of garlands to creat the appearance of a tree dressed in ornaments without having to hang them o by one. Draped branches have a playful design loaded with overlapping lines.

the tree tradition

What's your tree style? Eclectic? Contemporary? Traditional?
From themed trees to those full of surprises, each one is as unique
as the people who deck the branches.

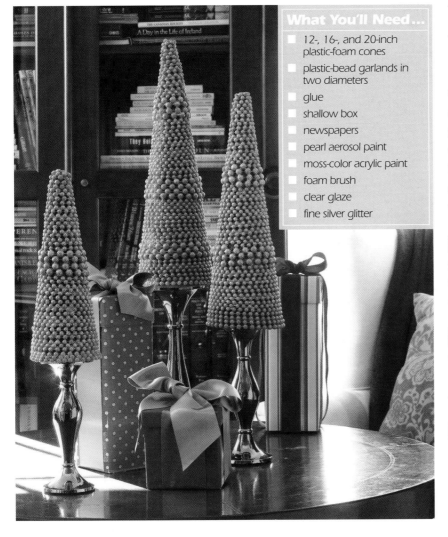

What You'll Need...

- ☐ 12-, 16-, and 20-inch plastic-foam cones
- ☐ plastic-bead garlands in two diameters
- ☐ glue
- ☐ shallow box
- ☐ newspapers
- ☐ pearl aerosol paint
- ☐ moss-color acrylic paint
- ☐ foam brush
- ☐ clear glaze
- ☐ fine silver glitter

bead-wrapped beauties

Beaded topiaries set on candlesticks lend holiday spirit to a table or mantel. Make trees by wrapping plastic-foam cones with beaded garland, then paint them to achieve luster. Wrapped packages in various sizes complete the vignette.

1 Beginning at the top, wrap and glue the plastic-bead garlands around each cone as shown in **Photo A,** alternating bead size. Let adhesive dry.

2 Line a shallow box with newspaper and place the cone in the box. Spray a base coat of pearl paint to prepare the surface for acrylic paint.

3 Mix two parts acrylic paint with one part water. Paint the cone, pressing the brush between the beads to apply paint to the foam base. Let paint dry. If needed, apply another coat of the paint mixture for solid coverage. Let dry. Apply glaze with a brush as shown in **Photo B.** Immediately sprinkle a heavy coat of glitter on wet glaze. Let dry.

A

B

What You'll Need...

- [ ] urn-style pot large enough for tree
- [ ] spray paint (optional)
- [ ] tree
- [ ] hedge clippers or heavy-duty pruning shears
- [ ] rocks, bricks, or wedges of wood to stabilize tree in pot
- [ ] towel
- [ ] ribbon for trunk and fence
- [ ] scissors
- [ ] duct tape
- [ ] wire cutters
- [ ] silk flowers
- [ ] small ball ornaments
- [ ] hot-glue gun and glue sticks
- [ ] beaded garland
- [ ] curling ribbon
- [ ] plastic ornamental garden fence
- [ ] handsaw
- [ ] clear tape
- [ ] decorative wired butterflies

blooms and butterflies

Spring has sprung in the still of winter. This happy-go-lucky tree warms the soul with bright, cheery colors and trendy details.

NOTE When purchasing a tree and urn, consider size and weight of each. The base of tree should fit easily and stand stable in the pot.

1 In a well-ventilated work area, spray-paint the urn. Let paint dry.

2 Using clippers or shears, trim off lower branches from tree, allowing approximately 12 inches of trunk to show in the urn.

3 Insert the tree into the urn, stabilizing it with rocks, small bricks, or wedges of wood. Wrap the trunk with a towel to help stand it straight and secure.

4 Wrap ribbon around the lower tree trunk, securing ribbon ends with duct tape.

5 Using wire cutters, trim the silk flower stems approximately 5 inches long.

6 Remove hangers from small ball ornaments. Hot-glue the balls to the flower centers. Glue balls and beaded garland to a large flower to make the topper.

7 Insert the flowers among the branches. Add strands of curled ribbon. If flower stems need to be held in place securely, use ribbon to tie them to branches.

8 For the fence, saw off the stakes meant to be inserted in the ground.

9 Weave ribbon through the fence and secure with clear tape if needed. Assemble around tree.

10 Tuck butterflies in among the tree branches and wire some to the fence.

41

in full bloom

Two-tone Strawberries 'n' Cream poinsettias are the ornaments on a potted tree-form topiary of English ivy. To use fresh blooms, cut the flowers with about 6 inches of stem. Remove the green leaves and a few outer clusters for petite blooms. Place the cut poinsettias in a vase of cool water for 30 minutes to allow cut ends to seal. Then poke each stem into a water-filled florist pick and nestle it into the ivy. Check water level daily; florist picks hold very little water. If kept moist, the poinsettias should stay fresh for two weeks or longer.

▶ No-Melt Snowmen

Won't the hardware store clerk be surprised that vent connectors are used to make snowmen? With a glittered plastic foam ball as the head, these guys sparkle with spirit. To give 'em personality, use upholstery tacks for eyes and mouths, screws for noses, and ribbon for scarves. For buttons, glue washers together and adhere to a small circle of felt. Glue a magnet to each felt piece and attach to metal vent.

In a Twinkling
heavenly hardware

▲ Chain Reaction

Buy chain by the foot to make a garland to hold mini ornaments, candy canes, jingle bells, or gift tags.

◀ Snow Globe

Breeze through the plumbing aisle and pick up a vent collar. Then off to the lighting section for a globe. Place a holiday tree inside and add stickers to the glass for a wintry scene.

Sillcock Snowflakes

Symmetrical metal handles lay the groundwork for artsy snowflakes. Use metal glue to attach a variety of washers. Once the glue is dry, spray on glitter to add extra shine.

43

Ruffled Candle Collar

Guests on the way? No problem! Make a jingle-jangle centerpiece in 2 minutes tops! Nest a 5-inch-diameter stovepipe collar in a 6-inch collar. Place a pillar candle in the center, fill with jingle bells, and tie a ribbon bow. Done!

Ductwork Wreath

Welcome guests with a hip wreath shaped from an 8-foot length of 3-inch-diameter flexible aluminum duct. Use an awl to pierce holes in duct ends and lace together with floral wire. Wrap the wreath with tinsel. Embellish with a ribbon bow and snowflake trim attached with floral wire.

a very berry Christmas

Holly sprigs, fresh evergreens, and vivid cranberries have the classic colors for holiday decorating that enliven table settings.

traditionally yours

❧ Cranberries floating above holly leaves and berries in a water-filled glass bowl encircle the centerpiece candle like a wreath. Evergreen branches and a cranberry garland enlarge the yuletide table decoration. At each place setting is a handful of berries beneath a floating candle. **Note:** Never leave burning candles unattended.

45

winter wool

Fashion homespun place mats and gift bags from layers of wool felt. Cut holly leaves in the red layer and sew felt circle "berries," then stitch the red layer to a green base.

What You'll Need...

- [ ] red and green felt
- [ ] scissors
- [ ] pins
- [ ] embroidery floss to match red felt
- [ ] sewing thread to match red felt
- [ ] embroidery needle
- [ ] sewing maching

1 For each place mat, cut a red felt rectangle a size that fits your table. Cut a green felt rectangle 1 inch larger on all sides.

2 Enlarge the holly leaf patterns on **page 155**; cut out the patterns. Pin the patterns to a corner of the red felt rectangle; cut out to make openings.

3 Cut ½-inch-diameter circles from red felt, tack them in place with red embroidery thread, tying knots with short tails on each berry. Trim the floss ends.

4 Use embroidery floss and needle to sew a running stitch through the center of each holly leaf.

5 Center the red wool layer on the green rectangle; topstitch the layers together.

berry cute

A simple loop of green grosgrain ribbon decorated with a berried holly sprig hugs silverware and a Christmas-red napkin.

goody bags

Scallop-edge layers of wool felt circles to make extra-special treat bags. Cinch them up tight with embellished ribbon and place one at each guest's plate.

the season's glow

Put lustrous shine on entertaining this Christmas with abundant candles.

falling snowflakes

❧ Secure mini snowflake ornaments to a red candle using white map pins. Use additional pins as polka dots. Set the candle in a white plate and fill with sparkling Epsom salts. For a pedestal, set the arrangement on a white soup bowl turned upside down.

Note: Never leave burning candles unattended.

poinsettia float

❧ Display poinsettias without obstructing the view across the dining table by clipping stems short and floating the clusters in a clear shallow bowl. To brighten the arrangement, press adhesive gems around the bowl lip. Add sparkle to floating candles by heating the tops with a hair dryer, then sprinkling them with silver glitter. To light the candles, place them in glasses surrounding but not touching the poinsettia blooms.

flower band votives

❧ Festive ribbon bands encircle votive candleholders for the holidays. Use a brad to attach paper poinsettia leaves to one end of velvet ribbon. Trim the ribbon to fit around the candleholder and use a glue dot to hold it in place.

frosted lantern

✺ Snowflake stencils offer a wintry design that lasts no matter what the climate.

1 Stencil snowflakes onto glass sides of lantern using purchased stencil and white craft paint.

2 Sprinkle glitter on wet paint; shake off excess. Let paint and glitter set.

3 Arrange candles and greenery inside lantern. Place lantern on the metallic plate.

4 Place mirrored balls and greenery around lantern base.

5 Tie jingle bells and a greenery sprig to the lantern top.

Note: Never leave burning candles unattended.

sparkling glow

✺ Nestle a chunky candle in a shallow glass dish. Fill the container halfway with aquarium pellets. Surround with assorted colorful ornaments.

- green stemmed dessert dishes and saucers
- white wax candle granules
- candle wicks
- scissors
- artificial berries

berry refreshing

Beaded red berries and pale green glassware are a fresh approach to holiday candles.

1 Pour wax granules in dessert dishes to approximately tho-thirds full.

2 For each candle, cut a wick long enough to extend 1 inch above granules; insert in center of mounded granules in dish.

3 Rest beaded berries along rims of dessert dishes, keeping all flammable materials away from wicks.

51

ribbon-wrapped candle

Towering in elegance, this pillar candle glistens with crossing bands of gold and green.

1 Cut three lengths of green ribbon long enough to wrap around candle with ends slightly overlapping. Evenly space ribbons around the candle near top, center, and bottom, securing ribbon ends wih mini brads.

2 Cut 12 lengths of gold ribbon one and a half times the distance between the top and bottom ribbons wrapped around the candle.

3 Evenly space six pairs of ribbons around the top green ribbon; secure with brads. Crisscross ribbon pairs and secure with brads to center ribbon around candle. Continue ribbon design to lower ribbon band; trim any excess length and secure with brads. Embellish the candle with a ribbon bow and place on candleholder.

- cream or white pillar candle
- ribbons in green and gold
- scissors
- gold mini brads
- gold pillar candleholder

outdoor decor

snowy fun

When not cruising the snow-covered hills, an old sled, trimmed with pine boughs, pinecones, and fruit, does double duty as a welcoming decoration next to the front door.

Discover charming ways to transform functional items—from bikes to baskets—into seasonal works of art.

colorful ride

For a playful display, wrap vintage-style outdoor bulbs on yesteryear's two-wheeler—from handlebars to spokes—then park it along a decorative wall or prop it against a fence.

53

fruitful feast

This red plaid picnic basket is as appetizing in winter as it is in summer. It's filled with twigs secured in florist's foam and adorned with frosted silk fruits and berries.

frosty wheelbarrow

❧ Stand a small evergreen tree in a wheelbarrow as a holiday accent for the yard. Wrap the tree with a string of lights to glow at night.

mail call

❧ Decorate streetside mailboxes with a generous spray of greenery, twigs, and colorful berries.

garden style

❧ A white bench dressed up with bouquets of silvered holly leaves, gilded berries, and ribbon bows invites passersby to sit a moment for holiday reflection. These arrangements also work magic on light fixtures, poles, fences, and gates.

▶ Ribbon Candy Delights

Enjoy calorie-free holiday candy. To make them, thread a needle with embroidery floss and knot one end. Using clear acrylic beads and 1-inch-wide paper strips, create the candy shape by placing two beads between each bend of the paper strip. Secure the top bead by running the floss through it twice, and make a loop for hanging.

In a Twinkling
ornaments

▲ Dazzling Snowflake

Fold a square of paper in half diagonally, then again. Make cuts on all sides. Open, press, and outline edges with crafts glue and glitter.

◀ Christmas Clutches

To craft purse ornaments, use the pattern on **page 154** to cut a shape from cardstock. Score folds on outside; fold. Paper- punch holes indicated. Glue trim along flap edge. Attach a beaded wire handle, bending ends to secure. Glue trim onto flap. For closure, add adhesive-backed hook-and-loop tape.

Three-Ring Circus

Form 1¼×7-inch-long strips of double-sided cardstock in rings. Overlap ends and use glue stick to secure. Punch a hole at overlap for the hanger. Knot the ends of narrow ribbon, slip on chunky wooden beads, and push the ribbon loop through the hole.

Befringed Evergreen

Cut 4½-inch triangles from scrapbook paper and cardboard. Cut a ¾×2-inch paper rectangle for trunk. Sandwich a thread loop and the trunk between the front and back; glue together. Using glue dots, adhere rows of lace and beaded fringe trims on tree shape. Top with a bead adhered with a glue dot.

No-Knit Mitt

Paper mittens are cute pockets for small goodies. To cut shapes, use the pattern on **page 154.** Join mitten front to back using embroidery floss and blanket stitches. Glue on cuff pieces, securing edges with cross-stitches; make a hanging loop.

See "Wee Winter Warm-Me-Ups", page 104.

GATHERING *together*

Celebrate the holidays with family and friends, sharing time, fond memories, delicious food, a welcoming home, and a cozy atmosphere.

59

Rosemary Beef Tenderloin,
recipe on page 68

60

build on holiday traditions

Present long-standing holiday favorites with enticing new recipe and decorating variations that spark the celebration into something unforgettable.

Here's How: Deveining Shrimp

Purchase fresh shrimp in the shells from a reputable seafood market, then peel and devein it yourself. Although peeling, deveining, and cooking yourself take a bit more time, the fresh rich taste is worth the effort. Here's how:

- Open the shell lengthwise down the body. Starting at the head end, peel back the shell. Gently pull on the tail to remove it.
- To devein, use a sharp knife to make a shallow slit along the back from head to tail end. Locate the black vein. Hold the shrimp under cold running water to rinse the vein away. Or use the tip of a knife to remove the vein, then rinse the shrimp.

Herbed Shrimp and Tomatoes

Herbed Shrimp and Tomatoes

✳

Shrimp cocktail has a modern appeal with grape tomatoes and herb sauce.

- 2 pounds fresh or frozen jumbo shrimp (40 to 42 shrimp)
- 2 tablespoons snipped fresh basil or oregano
- 1 tablespoon fresh lemon juice
- ¾ teaspoon salt
- ¼ teaspoon ground black pepper
- 2 tablespoons extra virgin olive oil
- 2 cups grape tomatoes
  Lemon wedges
  Snipped fresh basil
- 1 recipe Basil Dipping Sauce

Thaw shrimp, if frozen. Peel, devein, and remove tails. Rinse shrimp; pat dry with paper towels. Set aside. In large bowl combine basil, lemon juice, salt, and pepper. Add shrimp. Toss to coat. Cover and marinate in refrigerator for 10 to 30 minutes.

In a large skillet cook marinated shrimp, half at a time, in the hot olive oil over medium-high heat for 2 to 3 minutes or until shrimp are opaque, stirring often to cook evenly. Transfer shrimp to a serving platter.

Add tomatoes to shrimp on platter; gently toss to combine. Serve with lemon wedges, snipped basil, and Basil Dipping Sauce. Serve warm. Makes 8 servings.

BASIL DIPPING SAUCE

In a small bowl combine 1 cup mayonnaise; 1 tablespoon snipped fresh basil; 2 cloves garlic, minced; 1 teaspoon lemon juice; 1 teaspoon Dijon-style mustard; and ⅛ teaspoon cayenne pepper. Cover; chill up to 3 days before serving. Makes 1 cup.

MAKE-AHEAD DIRECTIONS

This dish is also great served chilled. Cover and refrigerate cooked shrimp mixture up to 4 hours before serving.

Sparkling Kumquat Salad

Sparkling Kumquat Salad

✳

Tossed green salad enjoys a seasonal update with kumquats—members of the citrus family. Serve it in a clear glass bowl to add extra sparkle to the table.

- 1 recipe Sparkling Vinaigrette
- 1 small fennel bulb
- 3 tablespoons walnut pieces, toasted
- 3 tablespoons pomegranate seeds*
- 6 cups torn mixed salad greens
- ¼ cup kumquats, seeded and sliced
- ⅛ teaspoon salt
  Dash freshly ground black pepper

Prepare Sparkling Vinaigrette; set aside. Remove leaves from fennel. Snip enough leaves to measure 1 tablespoon. In a small bowl combine 1 tablespoon fennel leaves, toasted walnuts, and pomegranate seeds. Add 2 teaspoons of the vinaigrette; toss gently to coat. Set aside.

Core and thinly slice fennel bulb. In a large bowl combine sliced fennel, greens, kumquats, salt, and pepper. Sprinkle with fennel leaf-walnut mixture. Serve with remaining vinaigrette. Makes 4 servings.

SPARKLING VINAIGRETTE

In a blender or small food processor combine ¼ cup seeded and coarsely chopped kumquat, ¼ cup chilled sparkling dry white wine or sparkling white grape juice, 2 tablespoons walnut oil, 1 quartered small shallot, ⅛ teaspoon salt, dash ground black pepper, and dash ground coriander. Cover and blend or process until nearly smooth.

***TEST KITCHEN TIP** To remove pomegranate seeds, cut fruit just through skin. Remove peel and break the fruit into sections. Handle the fruit in a bowl filled with water so the seeds float to the top. In the water the juice won't discolor your hands. Use fingers or a small spoon to separate the seeds from the membrane. Discard skin and membrane.

BBQ Spice-Rubbed
Turkey Breasts,
Onion-Thyme Gravy

BBQ Spice-Rubbed Turkey Breasts

✳

If you like, serve with oven-roasted fingerling potatoes.

- 2 3- to 3½-pound fresh or frozen bone-in turkey breast halves
  Nonstick cooking spray
- 2 tablespoons packed dark brown sugar
- 2 teaspoons paprika
- 2 teaspoons garlic powder
- 1½ teaspoons salt
- 1 teaspoon ground cumin
- 1 teaspoon chili powder
- ¾ teaspoon freshly ground black pepper
- 1 recipe Cranberry Barbecue Sauce or Onion-Thyme Gravy

Thaw turkey breasts, if frozen. Preheat oven to 400°F. Coat a large shallow roasting pan and rack with cooking spray. In a small bowl combine brown sugar, paprika, garlic powder, salt, cumin, chili powder, and pepper. Place turkey breast halves, bone sides down, on rack in prepared pan.

Starting at the breast bone, slip fingers between skin and meat to loosen skin, leaving skin attached at top. Lift skin and evenly spread spice mixture under skin over breast meat. Insert an oven-going meat thermometer into the thickest part of breast, without touching bone.

Roast, uncovered, on lower rack of oven for 20 minutes. Reduce oven temperature to 350°F and roast for 1 to 1½ hours longer or until thermometer registers 170°F, juices run clear, and turkey is no longer pink, occasionally spooning pan juices over turkey. Let stand, covered with foil, for 10 minutes before slicing. Place breast halves on platter. Serve with Cranberry Barbecue Sauce or Onion-Thyme Gravy. Makes 10 to 12 servings.

TEST KITCHEN TIP To simplify preparation, rub spice mixture onto outsides of turkey breasts for a crusty spice appearance. Place foil over turkey breast the last 30 minutes of roasting to prevent burning.

Cranberry Barbecue Sauce

✳

- 1 cup chopped onion (1 large)
- 1 tablespoon cooking oil
- 1 16-ounce can whole cranberry sauce
- ⅓ cup bottled chili sauce
- 1 tablespoon cider vinegar
- 1 teaspoon Worcestershire sauce
- ¼ teaspoon freshly ground black pepper

In a medium saucepan cook onion in hot oil over medium heat for 5 minutes. Add cranberry sauce, chili sauce, vinegar, Worcestershire sauce, and pepper. Bring to boiling; reduce heat. Simmer, uncovered, stirring occasionally, for 5 minutes or until thickened. Pass with BBQ Spice-Rubbed Turkey Breasts. Makes 10 to 12 (¼-cup) servings.

MAKE-AHEAD DIRECTIONS
Prepare the sauce as directed; cover and refrigerate up to 3 days. Reheat before serving.

Onion-Thyme Gravy

✳

For some, it just isn't a holiday meal without gravy. In this update shallots provide a deeply rich onion-garlic flavor.

- 2 tablespoons butter
- 1 cup chopped onion (1 large)
- 3 shallots, chopped (⅔ cup)
- 1 teaspoon snipped fresh thyme or ¼ teaspoon dried thyme, crushed
- 2 tablespoons all-purpose flour
- 1 14-ounce can reduced-sodium chicken broth
- 1 tablespoon reduced-sodium soy sauce
- 1 tablespoon Worcestershire sauce
- ¼ teaspoon freshly ground black pepper
- ⅛ teaspoon salt

In a medium saucepan melt butter over medium-high heat. Add the onion, shallots, and thyme. Cook, stirring occasionally, for 10 to 12 minutes or until vegetables are tender and browned.

Stir in flour; cook and stir for 1 minute. Add broth, soy sauce, and Worcestershire sauce. Cook and stir until broth mixture comes to boiling; reduce heat to medium. Simmer, uncovered, for 8 to 9 minutes or until slightly thickened. Stir in the pepper and salt. Makes 2¼ cups gravy.

Holiday Wine Choices

So many flavors, so many wines! How to pick the right bottle to go with holiday foods? First, it's a good idea to serve both a red and a white. Many people prefer one over the other, and even wine drinkers who enjoy both often prefer to kick off a meal with white, then move to red for the main course. A few more tips for approaching your wine selection:

- **By popular vote.** Chardonnay remains a favorite white, while Merlot is a top red. If you serve these two, you'll likely make most guests happy. Although Chardonnay goes better with seafood, chicken, and creamy dishes, in truth most Chard lovers enjoy the wine with whatever's being served. Merlot goes great with turkey, pork, and beef—so you're covered for holiday meals.
- **By food friendliness.** If you're looking for versatile "never let you down" wines to go with a great variety of foods, remember Pinot Grigio and Pinot Noir. Pinot Grigio is an easy-sipping wine that complements many foods. Pinot Noir is also famous for its go-with-anything qualities.

Pecan Cakes,
Raspberry-Cranberry Sauce

Pecan Cakes

✳

Freeze these minicakes up to one month. After serving, send extras home as party favors, wrapped in festive cellophane food gift bags.

- 1 cup butter, softened
- 1½ cups granulated sugar
- 2½ teaspoons baking powder
- 1 teaspoon vanilla
- ½ teaspoon salt
- 3 eggs
- 2¼ cups all-purpose flour
- ½ cup pecans, toasted and ground
- 1¼ cups milk
- Powdered sugar
- Fresh raspberries
- Fresh mint leaves
- 1 recipe Raspberry-Cranberry Sauce

Preheat oven to 350°F. Grease and flour twenty-four 2½-inch muffin cups; set aside.

In a large mixing bowl beat butter with an electric mixer on medium speed for 30 seconds. Gradually beat in granulated sugar until combined, scraping sides of bowl occasionally. Beat in baking powder, vanilla, and salt. Add eggs, 1 at a time, beating well after each addition.

In another large bowl combine flour and pecans. Alternately add flour mixture and milk to butter mixture, beating on low speed after each addition just until combined. Evenly spoon batter into prepared muffin cups.

Bake for 15 to 18 minutes or until a wooden toothpick inserted in centers comes out clean. Cool in pans on a wire rack for 5 minutes. Remove from pans. Cool completely on racks. Before serving, sprinkle with powdered sugar and garnish with raspberries and mint leaves. Serve with Raspberry-Cranberry Sauce. Makes 24 cakes.

Granny Smith and Smoked Cheddar Gratin

Raspberry-Cranberry Sauce

✳

This luscious topper for Pecan Cakes is also a delicious sauce over ice cream and pears—a refreshing finale to a holiday meal.

- 2 cups fresh or frozen cranberries
- ¼ cup golden raisins
- 1 cup sugar
- ¼ cup port or cranberry juice
- ½ teaspoon ground ginger
- 1 cup fresh or frozen raspberries
- 1 teaspoon finely shredded orange peel
- Finely shredded orange peel (optional)

In a medium saucepan combine cranberries and raisins. Stir in sugar, port or juice, and ginger. Cook and stir over medium heat until sugar is dissolved. Cook and stir 5 minutes more or until cranberries begin to pop and mixture is slightly thickened. Remove saucepan from heat.

Stir in raspberries and the 1 teaspoon orange peel. Serve with Pecan Cakes. If desired, top with additional orange peel. Makes about 2 cups sauce.

Granny Smith and Smoked Cheddar Gratin

✳

Holiday cooks have long appreciated au gratin potatoes. No last-minute mashing!

- 6 medium potatoes (2 pounds), peeled, if desired, and thinly sliced (about 6 cups)
- 2 large Granny Smith apples
- ½ cup chopped onion (1 medium)
- 2 large cloves garlic, minced
- 2 tablespoons olive oil
- ¼ cup all-purpose flour
- 1 teaspoon salt
- ¼ teaspoon ground black pepper
- 3 cups milk
- 2 teaspoons snipped fresh thyme
- 4 ounces smoked cheddar or Gouda cheese, shredded

Preheat oven to 350°F. Grease a 2½- to 3-quart au gratin or rectangular baking dish or two 1½-quart au gratin dishes; set aside. Cook potatoes in enough lightly salted boiling water to cover for 5 minutes. Drain; set aside. Core and cut apples into thin wedges; set aside.

For sauce, in a saucepan cook onion and garlic in hot oil over medium heat until tender. Stir in flour, salt, and pepper. Add milk all at once. Cook and stir until thickened and bubbly.

Remove from heat. Stir in thyme. In prepared dish or dishes layer half the potatoes and half the apples. Pour half the sauce over the potatoes and apples. Sprinkle with half the cheese. Repeat with remaining potatoes, apples, and sauce. Cover and refrigerate remaining cheese.

Bake, covered, for 35 minutes for large dish or 20 minutes for small dishes. Uncover. Top with remaining cheese. Bake for 35 minutes more or until potatoes are tender and top is golden. Let stand 10 minutes before serving. Makes 8 side-dish servings.

Rosemary Beef Tenderloin

✳

Ready to pull out all the stops? Count on beef tenderloin to dazzle. Goat cheese makes the entrée even more of an event. Shown on page 60.

      2 tablespoons Dijon-style mustard
      1 tablespoon extra virgin olive oil
      1 tablespoon snipped
          fresh rosemary
      3 cloves garlic, minced
    ¾ teaspoon salt
    ¼ teaspoon ground black pepper
      1 2½- to 3-pound center-cut beef
          tenderloin roast
      1 4- to 6-ounce log garlic and herb
          goat cheese (chèvre),
          cut crosswise into 8 slices,
          or ½ of an 8-ounce tub
          cream cheese spread with
          chive and onion
          Snipped fresh rosemary
          Garnishes (optional)

In a small bowl combine mustard, olive oil, the 1 tablespoon rosemary, garlic, salt, and pepper. Spread mixture on top of the beef. Place meat on a rack in a shallow roasting pan.

Preheat oven to 425°F. For medium-rare beef, roast meat, uncovered, for 35 to 40 minutes or until internal temperature of meat registers 135°F on an instant-read thermometer. Cover with foil; let stand 15 minutes before slicing. Meat temperature after standing should be 145°F. (For medium doneness, roast, uncovered, for 45 to 50 minutes or until meat reaches 150°F. Cover and let stand as directed above. Meat temperature should reach 160°F after standing.)

To serve, cut 8 slices in the roast about 1 to 1½ inches apart, cutting to, but not through, the bottom of the roast. Tuck a slice of goat cheese into each cut (or spoon 1 tablespoon cream cheese into each cut). Sprinkle with

Chile-Chocolate Torte with Cinnamon Whipped Cream

additional rosemary. To serve, slice through beef between each cheese portion. Makes 8 servings.

Chile-Chocolate Torte with Cinnamon Whipped Cream

✳

Chile pepper in cake? Indeed! Just a touch deepens the flavor of chocolate. Guests will be trying to guess the secret ingredient.

          Nonstick cooking spray
          All-purpose flour
      1 cup whole blanched almonds
      2 tablespoons granulated sugar
      2 tablespoons all-purpose flour
      1 pound Mexican-style sweet
          chocolate or 1 pound
          semisweet chocolate, coarsely
          chopped
      3 ounces semisweet chocolate,
          coarsely chopped
      1 cup butter
      6 egg yolks
    ¼ cup strong brewed coffee,
          cooled
      1 teaspoon vanilla
    ¼ teaspoon almond extract

    ½ teaspoon ground chipotle
          chile pepper or ¼ teaspoon
          cayenne pepper
    ¼ teaspoon ground cinnamon
      6 egg whites
    ¼ cup granulated sugar
      1 cup whipping cream
    ¼ cup powdered sugar
    ¼ teaspoon ground cinnamon
          Whole blanched, unblanched, or
          candied almonds
          Crushed chipotle chile pepper
          (optional)

Preheat oven to 325°F. Lightly coat a 9-inch springform pan with nonstick cooking spray; line bottom with parchment paper. Coat with cooking spray; sprinkle with flour and shake excess from pan. Set aside.

In a food processor combine the 1 cup almonds, 2 tablespoons granulated sugar, and 2 tablespoons flour. Cover and process until ground, 1 to 2 minutes.

In a large heavy saucepan combine Mexican-style chocolate, semisweet chocolate, and butter. Cook over low heat, stirring occasionally, until chocolate and butter are melted. Cool 5 minutes.

One Tree Three Ways

Aromatic rosemary trees are natural beauties for holiday tables. Pick up a tree at a grocery store or nursery to trim. Keep it watered and give it lots of light. Clip the fresh rosemary to enhance the flavor of meat or add a snip to cooked sauces or soups.

sprinkled with cinnamon

ℕ Tie red raffia around cinnamon sticks to tuck in branches along with a string of cranberries. Dress the pot by wrapping it with natural rope secured with hot glue.

Meanwhile, in a large bowl combine egg yolks, coffee, vanilla, almond extract, and ⅛ teaspoon salt. Stir in ground almond mixture, cooled chocolate mixture, ground chipotle chile pepper, and ¼ teaspoon cinnamon.

In another large mixing bowl beat egg whites with an electric mixer on high speed until soft peaks form. Gradually add the ¼ cup granulated sugar, beating until stiff peaks form, 1 to 2 minutes. Fold whites into chocolate mixture. Pour into the prepared pan.

Bake for 35 to 40 minutes or just until set. Transfer pan to rack; cool for 1 hour. (Center of cake will sink as it cools.) Refrigerate at least 3 hours.

To unmold cake, use a small sharp knife to loosen cake from sides of pan; remove sides of pan. Invert cake onto a plate; remove pan bottom and parchment paper. Invert cake onto a platter.

In a chilled mixing bowl combine whipping cream, powdered sugar, and ¼ teaspoon cinnamon. Beat until soft peaks form. Top cake with whipped cream. Sprinkle with almonds and, if desired, crushed chipotle chile pepper. Makes 12 to 16 servings.

the thrill of frill

ℕ Purchased ribbon bows and ball ornament picks decorate a tree elegantly. Simply poke the trims in the tree. If the tree sits in a foil wrapper, rest it in a bowl before watering.

sweet as can be

ℕ Nestle small candy canes in the tree, allowing only hooks to show. Fill in with red jingle bells twisted onto craft wire. Place the planter (or repot the tree) in a clean paint pail available from paint stores and home centers. Finish the tabletop tree with a red and white ribbon bow.

musical merriment

From church choirs echoing yuletide hymns to new renditions playing on the radio, holiday music is a year-end ritual we look forward to and savor. Share the love of music with grand decorating touches that are purely harmonious.

sheet music star

꙳ Add musical notes to a tree with quick-to-craft paper ornaments.

1 Trace the star pattern from **page 157**. Choose the solid outline for one of three sizes. Or make three copies to create small, medium, and large stars.

2 Trace outline of star pattern onto sheet music or scrapbook paper, positioning star in any direction on paper. Cut out star shape.

3 With the pattern as a guide, fold each star. Solid lines indicate "mountain folds" (fold toward you); dashed lines indicate "valley folds" (fold away from you).

4 Use a needle to punch a small hole as shown on the pattern. Thread a bead onto gold thread, slip one end through the hole, and knot the ends for a hanger.

make a grand entrance

Wrapped gifts add color to the entry hall, where a contrabass stands ready for a sing-along. Large instruments, such as this instrument or a guitar or drum set, state the music theme boldly. In place of an instrument, stand a book or sheet music prominently on a music stand.

a-caroling we will go

~ Gather sheet music in books for an evening of caroling or a sing-along around the piano.

72

What You'll Need...

- [ ] decorative upholstery or velvet
- [ ] presentation book with page sleeves or binder with sleeves
- [ ] scissors
- [ ] iron and ironing board (optional)
- [ ] newspaper
- [ ] spray adhesive
- [ ] E6000 adhesive
- [ ] toothpick
- [ ] decorative trim
- [ ] flat metal or plastic ornaments
- [ ] gold tieback curtain tassel
- [ ] sheet music

1 Lay fabric flat on work surface. Open and place presentation book flat on fabric. Trim fabric around book, leaving extra to be trimmed later. If necessary, iron fabric until smooth.

2 In a well-ventilated work area, lay opened book, covers face up, on newspaper-covered surface. Evenly spray a coat of adhesive across both covers. Let dry until tacky.

3 Carefully lay fabric on adhesive-coated book, smoothing evenly. Press firmly to adhere fabric to book.

4 Use scissors to trim excess fabric from cover edges.

5 Using a toothpick and E6000 adhesive, glue decorative trim, beginning at binding and adhering all around the edge of the book. Trim off ends. Adhere ornaments to the book cover.

6 Open book to center. Place tassel and trim tieback to desired length. Dab a small amount of E6000 adhesive to tassel end to prevent fraying.

7 Insert sheet music into pages.

well orchestrated

Incorporate musical instruments into holiday centerpieces. A colorful music book, glistening fruit picks, sprays of greenery, and metallic sheer ribbon perform a chic ensemble. In place of a case to hold the arrangement, a wooden box, small hard-side suitcase, or a wrapped box bottom can provide support.

73

keeping time

〜 Decorate a clock with a tiny musical arrangement. Tie a large plaid ribbon bow around the clock, tuck in artificial greenery, top with a small contrasting bow, and prop an instrument ornament in place with a tiny ball of poster adhesive.

you're invited

〜 A visit to the scrapbook store and you're on the way to making melodious party invitations. Choose dimensional instrument stickers to place front and center on layers of music-theme papers cut in proportion to ready-made note cards. These noteworthy cards also make great gift tags and gift-card assortments.

North Woods Christmas

Homespun crafts and decorations convey cozy warmth and invite relaxation. To update traditional red and green, blend bright accents of orange, pink, blue, and chartreuse with worn, time-honored accessories.

woodsy pinecones

Take a sack on your next hike through the woods. Fallen pinecones are wonderful additions to holiday trees. To cleanse pinecones, rinse with a weak water-bleach mixture and let dry. Twist an eye hook into one end, blanket the edges with spray snow, and tie on a ribbon bow.

bottle cozies

✺ If you've made Christmas stockings from sweaters, save those sleeves. Use them to dress holiday bottles. Turn under raw edges of sleeves and cinch with yarn around bottle necks. For coasters, tack two sizes of felt squares together with floss using simple embroidery stitches.

color-swirl ornaments

✺ Add some fun to each place setting with a colorful rolled-felt ornament. Cut ½-inch-wide felt strips, layer, and roll into a circle. Slip a felt strip in the center and knot at the top. Booties adorned with buttons become playful silverware holders.

candlelight dinner

Warm your holiday table with a candlescape of color inspired by striped knit scarves that serve as a tablecloth. Place tall candles in the center with small pillars surrounding. If you plan to light the candles, choose unscented varieties so aromas won't clash. **Note:** Never leave burning candles unattended.

knit whit

ꙮ **Recycling is frugal and fashionable. Worn sweaters and outerwear find new purpose when decorated as one-of-a-kind stockings.**

What You'll Need...

- tracing paper
- pencil
- scissors
- cotton sweaters
- sewing needle (optional)
- matching thread
- felt to coordinate with sweater
- fusible webbing
- buttons (optional)
- crochet hook (optional)
- sewing machine
- chenille yarn in 3 colors to coordinate with sweater
- hot-glue gun; glue sticks

1 Trace the stocking pattern on **page 155** onto tracing paper. Cut out the pattern.

2 Use the pattern to cut one stocking front from sweater. If using part of a sweater with buttons, use sewing thread and needle to tack opening closed. For a cuff, such as on the fringed version, add 3 to 4 inches of sweater at top of pattern. From felt cut out a lining and a back. Cut one stocking shape from fusible webbing.

3 Following manufacturer's instructions, fuse stocking front to one felt lining piece using fusible webbing.

4 Sew decorative trims, such as buttons, pom-poms, and fringe, to stocking fronts. To add fringe, use a crochet hook to pull yarn loops through cuff edge.

5 Sew stocking front to back around the edges, using a ¼-inch seam and leaving the top open.

braided-band tree skirt

❧ Chenille yarns distinctively outline a ready-made red and white tree skirt. Use four strands each of three yarn colors to braid the band. Attach with a hot-glue gun.

bountiful basket

❧ Small gifts or empty boxes present a lovely holiday accent grouped in a pretty pinecone-edged basket. Tuck in a few evergreen clippings for color, freshness, and texture.

6 For braided edging, cut approximately four 2-yard lengths from each of three yarn colors. Knot yarn ends together, leaving a 2-inch tail. Braid yarn strands, keeping like colors together and making the braid long enough to extend around stocking edges. Knot yarn ends; trim, leaving a 2-inch tail. Knot two yarn tails on heel side of stocking for a hanger.

7 Hot-glue braided yarn to stocking edge.

falling snowflakes throw

A simple felting technique embellishes a warm wool throw with colorful snowflakes. Make them sparkle with beaded accents sewn to the edges of the oversize patterns.

What You'll Need...

- [ ] tracing paper
- [ ] pencil
- [ ] scissors
- [ ] colorful wool felt
- [ ] needle felting tool and mat
- [ ] cream-color wool throw
- [ ] craft beads
- [ ] plaid wool fabric for binding
- [ ] sewing needle and thread

1 Trace the snowflake patterns on **page 155.** Use the patterns to cut snowflakes from wool felt. Cut as many as desired for the throw.

2 Using directions on the needle felting tool and mat package, felt snowflakes to random positions on throw, using the photo as a guide.

3 Using needle and thread, embellish snowflakes with craft beads.

4 Bind throw edges with bias-cut plaid wool fabric in desired width.

looking-glass trims

Let photos personalize tree branches. Black-and-white photos from any era deliver old-world charm.

What You'll Need...

- [ ] plastic pull-apart ornaments (available year-round in crafts stores)
- [ ] black-and-white photos
- [ ] pencil
- [ ] scissors
- [ ] circle cutter
- [ ] cardstock in green, red, and silver
- [ ] glue stick
- [ ] silver glass seed beads in large and small sizes
- [ ] hot-glue gun and glue sticks
- [ ] silver chenille stems
- [ ] jingle bells in red and green
- [ ] fine-tip marking pen (optional)

1 Take apart ornament. Use one half for each looking-glass ornament.

2 Place ornament half on photograph to frame desired image. Trace around ornament. Cut out photograph on drawn line.

3 Using a circle cutter, cut a cardstock circle ½ inch larger in diameter than the photograph. Cut a silver circle ¼ inch larger in diameter than the cardstock.

4 Use glue stick to adhere the photograph and two cardstock circles. Place a small pile of beads in the center.

5 Center the ornament half on the circles. Secure using a line of hot glue around ornament edge. Make a hanging loop in the center of a chenille stem, twisting to secure. Cover the line of glue by hot-gluing chenille stem around the ornament. If necessary, cut additional chenille stem to cover the glue; set in place.

6 Hot-glue two jingle bells to the ornament top. If desired, record information about the photograph on the back of the ornament.

festive Italian finales

Cannoli, recipe on page 86

Present a taste of
la dolce vita
at the table with
lavish Italian
desserts. Whether
you crave rustic or
elegant, you'll find
the perfect finish to
holiday celebrations.

Zuppa Inglese Parfaits, recipe on page 88

85

Cannoli

✳

Cannoli (ka-NO-lee) are quintessential Sicilian treats. With sweetened cheese, bittersweet chocolate, and rich pistachio nuts, this version has Italian flavor in every bite. Shown on page 84.

  1 15-ounce carton ricotta cheese
  ¾ cup powdered sugar
  1 teaspoon vanilla
  1 ounce bittersweet or semisweet chocolate, grated
  4 ounces bittersweet or semisweet chocolate, chopped
  1 tablespoon shortening
  12 purchased cannoli shells
  ¾ cup finely chopped pistachio nuts
  1 cup whipping cream

For filling, in a medium bowl stir together ricotta cheese, powdered sugar, and vanilla until almost smooth. Stir in the 1 ounce grated bittersweet chocolate. Cover and refrigerate filling up to 6 hours.

Meanwhile, in a small saucepan heat and stir the 4 ounces chopped bittersweet chocolate and the shortening over low heat until melted. Remove from heat. Transfer to a small bowl. Dip both ends of the cannoli shells in chocolate, letting excess drip off. Sprinkle chocolate ends with pistachio nuts. Arrange on a wire rack placed over waxed paper to set (about 45 minutes).

When chocolate is set, in a medium mixing bowl beat whipping cream on medium speed of an electric mixer or with a wire whisk until stiff peaks form. Fold into the ricotta mixture. Spoon filling into a decorating bag fitted with a large round or open star tip (or spoon into a resealable plastic bag; seal bag and snip off a small corner of the bag). Pipe filling into shells. Cover and refrigerate up to 2 hours. Makes 12 servings.

CHOCOLATE CANNOLI Prepare Cannoli as directed, except stir ¼ cup unsweetened cocoa powder into the ricotta mixture.

MAKE-AHEAD DIRECTIONS Dip unfilled cannoli shells in chocolate and sprinkle with nuts; store in an airtight container up to 3 days.

Layered Chocolate-Zabaglione Cream Cakes

✳

Zabaglione (zah-bahl-YOH-nay) is a light custard made with wine or liqueur. Traditionally it's made right before serving.

  6 eggs
  ½ cup unsalted butter
  3 ounces bittersweet chocolate
  1 cup granulated sugar
  2 teaspoons vanilla
  ½ teaspoon ground cinnamon
  1 cup sifted cake flour
  1 recipe White Chocolate Cream Frosting
  1 recipe White Chocolate Zabaglione Sauce
     Chocolate shavings (optional)

Allow eggs to stand at room temperature for 30 minutes. Grease a 15×10×1-inch baking pan. Line bottom with parchment paper or waxed paper; grease paper. Set aside. In a small saucepan combine butter and bittersweet chocolate. Stir over low heat until melted; set aside to cool.

Preheat oven to 350°F. In a large mixing bowl beat eggs slightly. Add sugar, vanilla, and cinnamon; beat with an electric mixer on high speed for 10 minutes. Sift about one-third of the flour over egg mixture; gently fold in. Repeat sifting and folding in one-third of the flour at a time. Gently fold in cooled melted chocolate mixture. Spread batter in prepared pan.

Bake for 18 to 20 minutes or until a wooden toothpick inserted near the center comes out clean. Cool cake in pan on a wire rack for 10 minutes. Remove cake from pan, invert, and peel off paper. Cool cake completely on a wire rack. Cut cake into twenty-four 2- to 2¼-inch circles or squares.

Just before serving, place half the cake circles or squares on a serving platter. On each cake, spread about 3 tablespoons of the White Chocolate Cream Frosting. Top each with a second cake. Spoon White Chocolate Zabaglione Sauce over cakes to drizzle over sides. If desired, garnish with chocolate shavings. Makes 12 servings.

WHITE CHOCOLATE CREAM FROSTING In a large mixing bowl beat ¾ cup whipping cream, ¼ cup powdered sugar, and 1 tablespoon white chocolate liqueur or clear crème de cacao with an electric mixer on high speed until stiff peaks form (tips stand straight). Use immediately.

WHITE CHOCOLATE ZABAGLIONE SAUCE In the top of a double boiler beat 4 egg yolks with ¼ cup white chocolate liqueur or clear crème de cacao, ¼ cup granulated sugar, and dash salt. Place over boiling water (upper pan should not touch water). Beat with an electric mixer on medium speed until mixture nearly triples in volume and temperature of mixture reaches 145°F and maintains that temperature for 3½ minutes (about 15 minutes total). Remove from heat. Place pan in a bowl of ice water; continue beating until zabaglione has cooled. In a small bowl beat ½ cup whipping cream with mixer on medium speed until soft peaks form. By hand, fold about one-fourth of the whipped cream into zabaglione; fold in remaining whipped cream.

Layered Chocolate-Zabaglione Cream Cakes

Zuppa Inglese Parfaits

✳

Zuppa inglese (zoo-pah ihn-GLAY-zay) translates to "English soup" from Italian. Some versions resemble trifle; others are like cake. This take layers hallmark ingredients—sponge cake, custard, spirits, candied fruits, and nuts—into irresistible individual parfaits. Shown on page 85.

- 2 eggs
- 1 recipe Custard Cream
- 1 cup all-purpose flour
- 1 teaspoon baking powder
- 1 cup sugar
- ½ cup milk
- 2 tablespoons butter
- 2 tablespoons rum
- 2 tablespoons cherry, apricot, or apple brandy
- ⅓ cup chopped candied fruits and peels
- ⅔ cup whipping cream
- 2 tablespoons sliced almonds, toasted

Allow eggs to stand at room temperature 30 minutes. Meanwhile, prepare Custard Cream. Cover surface with plastic wrap; refrigerate.

Preheat oven to 350°F. Lightly grease the bottom of a 9×1½-inch round cake pan. Line bottom of pan with waxed paper. Grease and lightly flour paper and sides of pan; set aside. In a small bowl stir together flour and baking powder; set aside.

In a mixing bowl beat the eggs with an electric mixer on high speed about 4 minutes or until thick. Gradually add sugar, beating on medium speed for 4 to 5 minutes or until light and fluffy. Add the flour mixture; beat on low to medium speed just until combined. In a small saucepan heat and stir the milk and butter until butter is melted; add to batter, beating until combined. Spread batter in prepared pan.

Bake 30 minutes or until a wooden toothpick inserted near center comes out clean. Cool in pan on wire rack 10 minutes. Remove from pan; cool.

To assemble, cut or tear cake into 1-inch pieces. Mix rum and brandy; divide half of the cake among eight parfait glasses. Sprinkle with half of the rum-brandy mixture, then half of the candied fruits and peels. Repeat layers. Carefully pour Custard Cream over cake. Cover and refrigerate parfaits up to 6 hours.

Just before serving, whip cream to stiff peaks. Top parfaits with whipped cream; sprinkle with almonds. Makes 8 servings.

CUSTARD CREAM In a heavy saucepan bring 1⅓ cups whipping cream just to boiling, stirring frequently. Remove from heat. In a mixing bowl stir a small amount of the hot cream into 2 egg yolks; add ⅔ cup sugar. Beat with an electric mixer on high speed for 2 to 3 minutes or until thick and lemon color. Gradually stir about half of the remaining cream into the egg yolk mixture. Return all of the egg yolk mixture to the saucepan. Cook and stir over medium heat just until mixture coats a metal spoon. Remove from heat. Stir in 1 teaspoon vanilla. Cover surface with plastic wrap. Chill in refrigerator; do not stir.

Country Pear and Blackberry Jam Crostata

✳

Chilling the dough makes it easier to roll out for the lattice topper. Brushing the lattice strips with milk and sprinkling with sugar promotes even browning.

- 2 cups all-purpose flour
- ⅓ cup granulated sugar
- 1½ teaspoons baking powder
- ⅔ cup butter
- 1 egg, lightly beaten
- ¼ cup milk
- 2 teaspoons finely shredded lemon peel
- 1 teaspoon vanilla
- ¾ cup blackberry preserves or jam
- 4 cups thinly sliced, peeled ripe pears (about 4 medium)
- ¼ cup granulated sugar
- 2 tablespoons butter, melted
  Milk
  Coarse sugar
  Lemon peel twists (optional)

Preheat oven to 375°F. In a medium bowl stir together the flour, the ⅓ cup granulated sugar, and baking powder. Using a pastry blender, cut in the ⅔ cup butter until mixture resembles coarse crumbs. Make a well in the center of the flour mixture.

In a small bowl stir together egg, the ¼ cup milk, 1 teaspoon of the lemon peel, and the vanilla. Pour milk mixture into flour mixture, stirring until moistened. Turn dough out onto a lightly floured surface and knead gently for 10 to 12 strokes or until smooth. Wrap one-third of the dough in plastic wrap and refrigerate.

Pat remaining dough into the bottom and up the sides of a 10-inch tart pan with a removable bottom. Evenly spread blackberry preserves over pastry in pan.

In a large bowl toss together the pears, the ¼ cup granulated sugar, and the remaining 1 teaspoon lemon peel. Arrange pear slices on preserves in tart pan. Drizzle with melted butter.

On a lightly floured surface, roll chilled pastry into a 10-inch circle. Cut into ½-inch-wide strips. Arrange strips over pears in a lattice pattern. Trim strips to edges of pan. Brush lattice with additional milk. Sprinkle with coarse sugar.

Bake for 45 to 50 minutes or until pears are tender. If necessary, to prevent overbrowning, loosely cover with foil during the last 10 minutes of baking. Cool in tart pan for 30 minutes. Remove tart from pan. If desired, garnish with lemon peel twists. Cut into wedges and serve warm. Makes 10 servings.

Country Pear and
Blackberry Jam Crostata

89

To Drink with Dessert

Add festive flair to the dessert course with these enticing sips from Italy.

Vin Santo: Shimmering like liquid amber in the glass, this thick, lightly sweet dessert wine, brimming with the flavors of caramel, spice, and dried and candied fruits, pairs especially well with caramel and nutty desserts. Biscotti dipped in Vin Santo is a classic finish to an Italian meal. Serve the delicacy cool, not ice cold, in small glasses.

Limoncello: This intensely lemony liqueur—at once both sweet and tart—has a brisk flavor that can perk up the palate at the end of a meal. It's better served after dessert than with it. Serve well chilled in small chilled liqueur glasses or shot glasses. Remember—it's meant for sipping.

Almond Panna Cotta with Mocha Sauce

✳

Panna Cotta has made quite the splash on restaurant dessert trays in recent years. This one can be made a day in advance.

 1 cup whole blanched almonds, toasted
 ⅔ cup sugar
 1 envelope unflavored gelatin
 2 cups whipping cream
 ½ cup milk
 ⅛ teaspoon salt
 1 recipe Mocha Sauce
  Toasted sliced almonds

Place whole almonds in a food processor and process until finely ground into a smooth butter. Set aside. **In a medium saucepan** stir together sugar and gelatin. Add cream. Heat and stir until gelatin is dissolved. Remove from heat. Stir in milk, salt, and almond butter. Pour cream mixture into six molds or 6-ounce ramekins or custard cups. Cover and refrigerate for 6 to 24 hours or until set. Make Mocha Sauce.

To serve, spoon some of the Mocha Sauce onto six dessert plates. Run a small clean kitchen knife around edge of mold to release the vacuum. Invert a molded dessert onto each plate. Serve with additional Mocha Sauce; sprinkle with sliced almonds. Makes 6 servings.

MOCHA SAUCE In a small heavy saucepan heat and stir 4 ounces chopped bittersweet or semisweet chocolate over low heat until melted. Stir in ⅔ cup whipping cream, ¼ cup sugar, and 1 teaspoon instant espresso coffee powder or regular instant coffee crystals. Cook and stir over medium-low heat about 3 minutes or until mixture just comes to boiling around the edges. Remove from heat. Cool for 15 minutes before serving. To store, cover and refrigerate up to 3 days. Makes about 1 cup sauce.

Almond Panna Cotta with Mocha Sauce

Cornmeal-Apple Cake

Cornmeal-Apple Cake

✳

Serve this dessert throughout autumn and winter. Apples and raisins are flavors of these seasons, and cornmeal adds a delightfully warm and rustic appeal to the cake.

 ¼ cup butter
 3 cups peeled, cored, and sliced baking apples (about 3 medium)
 ⅓ cup golden raisins
 2 tablespoons granulated sugar
 1 teaspoon ground cinnamon
 ¾ cup yellow cornmeal
 ¾ cup all-purpose flour
 2 teaspoons baking powder
 ½ teaspoon salt
 ¾ cup butter, softened
 1 cup granulated sugar
 1 teaspoon vanilla
 4 eggs
 ⅓ cup dairy sour cream
 1 tablespoon milk
  Powdered sugar

Preheat oven to 350°F. Grease the bottom and sides of a 9-inch springform pan; set aside. In a large skillet melt the ¼ cup butter over medium heat. Add apples and raisins. Cook about 8 minutes or just until apples are tender, stirring occasionally.

Remove from heat. Stir together the 2 tablespoons sugar and the cinnamon; stir into apple mixture. Reserve a few apple slices for garnish; refrigerate. Set aside remaining apple mixture.

In a medium bowl stir together cornmeal, flour, baking powder, and salt; set aside. In a large mixing bowl beat the ¾ cup butter with an electric mixer on medium to high speed for 30 seconds. Add the 1 cup sugar and the vanilla; beat until combined. Add eggs, 1 at a time, beating well after each. Add sour cream and milk; beat until combined. Fold in cornmeal mixture.

Pour two-thirds of the batter into the prepared pan. Add the apple mixture, arranging evenly on top of the batter. Pour remaining batter over apples; spread evenly.

Bake about 40 minutes or until a wooden toothpick inserted near the center comes out clean. Cool in pan on a wire rack for 20 minutes. Remove sides of pan and cool 20 minutes more.

To serve, use a serrated knife to cut warm cake into wedges. Place wedges on dessert plates. Sprinkle with powdered sugar and top with reserved apples. Makes 12 servings.

90

Triple-Chocolate Tiramisu

✳

It's surprising that tiramisu (tih-rah-mee-SOO) hasn't already become a classic holiday dessert. The light-as-air texture is just right after a rich meal.

2   3-ounce packages
    ladyfingers, split
¼   cup brewed espresso or
    strong coffee
1   8-ounce carton
    mascarpone cheese
1   cup whipping cream
¼   cup powdered sugar
1   teaspoon vanilla
⅓   cup chocolate liqueur
1   ounce white chocolate baking
    squares or white baking
    bars, grated
1   ounce bittersweet chocolate,
    grated
    Halved strawberries and/or
    raspberries
    Spearmint leaves

Line bottom of an 8×8×2-inch baking pan with some of the ladyfingers, cutting to fit. Drizzle half the espresso over ladyfingers. Set aside.

In a medium mixing bowl beat together mascarpone, whipping cream, powdered sugar, and vanilla with an electric mixer just until stiff peaks form. Beat in chocolate liqueur just until combined. Spoon half the mascarpone mixture over ladyfingers, spreading evenly. Sprinkle half the white chocolate and bittersweet chocolate over the mascarpone mixture. Top with another layer of ladyfingers (reserve any remaining ladyfingers for another use). Layer with remaining espresso, mascarpone cheese mixture, and grated chocolate.

Cover and refrigerate for 6 to 24 hours. Cover any leftovers and refrigerate up to 1 day. Garnish with berries and spearmint leaves. Makes 12 servings.

Triple-Chocolate Tiramisu

merry and bright

Vivid colors launch contemporary holiday decorating. Pinks, greens, blues, and oranges make a bold statement alongside winter white.

tabletop fiesta

☙ Punch up the table with yards of batik fabric. Keep the vibrant theme going with accessories such as votive candleholders, a tabletop ornament tree, and a matching wreath.

93

What You'll Need...

- ⅛-inch-wide bright-color ribbons
- scissors
- gold jewelry wire
- red round beads
- green oblong faceted beads
- hot-glue gun and glue sticks
- napkin rings in bright colors

holly bead napkin rings

☙ Reflect the intense color scheme at each place setting with decorative napkin rings.

1 For each napkin ring cut a 7-inch length of ribbon. Tie the ribbon in a bow.

2 Cut a 12-inch length of jewelry wire. String three red beads onto the wire; secure in the center by twisting wire ends together. One at a time, string green beads and fasten to red beads by twisting wire. Twist the two ends of wire together to secure. Trim excess wire and bend the ends into the center of a bead.

3 Using hot glue, adhere a ribbon bow to each napkin ring, then glue a beaded holly to the center of each bow.

center of attention

Trees are traditionally the focus in holiday decorating. This year make one shine with brilliant satin balls, hand-cut dimensional snowflakes, and a ball garland swagged across the branches.

dancing snowflakes

👐 Showy two-sided scrapbook papers make a dramatic statement on a white tree. Make the snowflakes in five easy-to-cut sections, then string together to complete.

1 Trace the quarter-circle pattern on **page 157**. Use the pattern to cut five wedge shapes from scrapbook paper.

2 With a crafts knife, cut along the lines indicated. Fold the sections away from center, alternating directions. Curl sections together and attach the points with glue dots or tape. Repeat for each of the five wedge shapes.

3 Attach five curled sections together at outer edge and center with a glue dot or tape. Thread a 7-inch length of gold thread through the top of the ornament and tie ends together.

beaded fabric garland

👐 Carry the batik look from tabletop to tree with a garland of the same fabric.

1 Cut a 5-inch-wide strip of fabric in the length desired for the garland.

2 Place a bead in the center of fabric strip; wrap fabric around bead. Slide fabric through a gold jump ring to secure bead. Alternate wrapping beads and slipping on rings the length of the fabric.

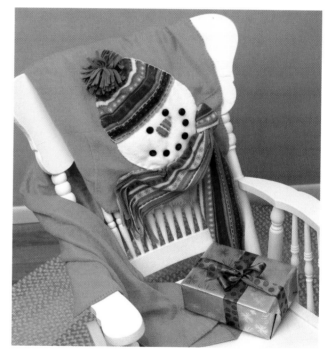

jolly throw

👐 Ward off winter chill with a cozy fleece throw that takes just an hour to make using a purchased fleece throw, a hat, and a scarf. Cut the hat in half. Cut a circle of white fleece to fit the hat. Hand- or machine-stitch the hat and face on the throw; tack on a nose, button eyes, and a mouth. Drape and stitch the scarf.

color-struck stockings

 Santa will be sure to fill these Christmas stockings of brilliant felt fleece. Beribboned or appliquéd, the stockings add magic at the hearth.

NOTE Felt cannot withstand a hot iron. Place a press cloth between the fabric and iron to prevent damaging the felt. Follow directions for the felting needle tool and mat to felt wool yarn to the stocking front. In lieu of felting tools, machine-zigzag yarn to the fabric.

1 Trace the stocking pattern on **page 158**. Cut out the pattern. Trace and cut out star patterns.

2 Fold fabric in half lengthwise. Using stocking pattern, cut front and back.

3 For ribbon stocking, pin ribbon lengths on stocking front for a cuff, heel, and toe as shown. Sew along edge of each ribbon to attach to stocking front. Place stocking front and back together, wrong sides facing. Machine-stitch a ½-inch seam allowance around stocking edges, leaving top open at cuff.

What You'll Need...

- scissors
- foam cones
- orange crafting foam
- straight pins
- play balls in 2 sizes
- low-temp glue gun and glue sticks
- ½- and 1-inch-diameter black buttons
- round foam rings, bowls, or cake pans
- large metal or plastic band bracelets, or canning jar rings
- wide ribbon, earmuffs, hats, or other accessories
- lightweight ornaments (optional)

cheery guys and gals

With contagious grins, these snowpeople take color to heart.

1 Cut off 3 inches of foam cone for nose. Wrap with orange crafting foam, cutting to fit; secure with straight pins.

2 Glue the orange foam nose on the small ball. Adhere button eyes and mouth above and below the nose.

3 Place the large ball in a ring, bowl, or pan. Set the bracelet or jar ring on the large ball; place the head on top. Secure with glue if needed.

4 Loop ribbon between the balls. Place earmuffs or a hat on the head; trim with lightweight ornaments.

4 For star stocking, follow directions for fusible webbing to adhere webbing on the cotton batik fabric. Cut out star shapes and peel paper off the fusible webbing. Follow directions on fusible webbing package to fuse stars to stocking front. Machine-satin-stitch or zigzag-stitch the edges of each star to secure to stocking front. Follow directions for felting needle tool to adhere yarn lengths as shown. Place front and back stocking pieces together, wrong sides facing. Sew ½-inch seam allowance. Machine-stitch around stocking, leaving the top of the stocking open at the cuff.

5 For both stockings, trim sewn edges with decorative-edge scissors or rotary cutter pinking blade. Do not pink cuff edges. Turn under the edge of the cuff ¼ inch and machine-stitch around it. For a hanger, cut a 1×6-inch length of felt or use a 6-inch length of ribbon and fold in half. Sew to inside of the heel side of the cuff.

tradition with a twist of lime

Drape your home in natural elegance with
the fresh combo of black, white, and lime green.

warm welcome

Holiday cheer begins at the front door.
Trim your stoop with a large square wreath,
fresh garland, and apple-filled urns. Apples
also ornament a pair of pine trees that flank
the steps.

sweet aroma

Fresh greenery scents the house
with pine. White roses resting in
water-filled vials provide even more
pleasant fragrance.

freshly wrapped

~ Greenery and sparkled pinecones secured with polka-dot ribbon are seasonal gift toppers.

harlequin ball

~ An artistic mix of black and white with harlequin chartreuse ornaments accents this graphic tree.

a step up

~ A vintage ladder supports greenery-stuffed, high-fashion stockings for a dramatic display.

hues of winter

Tall ceilings invite large-scale decorations. In this voluminous room, a 15-foot tree with 47 strands of white lights fills a corner. The massive wreath-topped mirror, directly on the mantel, is a backdrop for additional art. Greenery and chartreuse color the white spaces naturally.

greenhouse gathering

Set the stage for casual gatherings. Cover a table with no-frills burlap and dress the room with armloads of fresh greenery along with accents of green, black, and white.

sitting pretty

❧ Back each dining chair with a swag of fresh boxwood and Western cedar, all tied up with gingham ribbon.

table talk

❧ With a generous gathering of greenery as a base, potted topiaries and frost-tipped pinecones along with stems of fresh calla lilies carry out the black-and-white theme with accents of chartreuse.

still life

❧ Expanses of wall space are opportunities to expand holiday decor. This tableau displays a boxwood wreath hung from an old window frame, mophead hydrangeas, an apothecary jar of glass balls, and an ornate candelabra.

Cranberry-Pear Toddy,
Hot Apple-Raspberry Cider

'Tis the season
to welcome everyone in
from the cold with
irresistibly warm libations!

wee winter

Cranberry-Pear Toddy

✳

Two of winter's most beloved fruits star in this creative and elegant cupful.

- 3 cups cranberry nectar or cranberry juice
- 4 ounces pear brandy
- 4 ounces Cointreau or orange liqueur
  Fresh cranberries
- 4 lemon wedges (optional)

In a large saucepan heat the cranberry nectar over low to medium-low heat until simmering (do not boil). Remove from heat; add pear brandy and Cointreau.

Pour juice mixture into four heatproof punch cups or mugs. Garnish with a cocktail pick threaded with cranberries. If desired, garnish with a lemon wedge. Makes 4 (8-ounce) servings.

Hot Apple-Raspberry Cider

✳

With cognac and raspberry liqueur, this is a very sophisticated rendition of apple cider!

- 3 cups apple cider
- 1 tablespoon finely shredded orange peel
- 1/8 teaspoon ground cinnamon
- 1/8 teaspoon ground cloves
- 1/8 teaspoon ground cardamom
- 1 cup cognac
- 1/3 cup raspberry liqueur, such as Chambord
  Whipped cream
  Ground cinnamon
  Finely shredded orange peel

In a small saucepan combine the cider, orange peel, cinnamon, cloves,

Hot Cider Surprise Punch

and cardamom. Heat until steam rises from the surface (do not boil). Strain through a fine-mesh sieve to remove orange peel. Return to pan to heat through, if necessary.

Remove from heat; stir in the cognac and liqueur. Pour the hot cider into six heatproof cups or mugs. Garnish with whipped cream, additional cinnamon, and orange peel. Makes 6 (about 7-ounce) servings.

Hot Cider Surprise Punch

Brisk pomegranate juice adds deep color and sparkle to this flavorful sipper.

- 4 cups apple cider
- 4 cups cranberry juice
- 2 cups pomegranate juice
- 6 inches stick cinnamon
- 3 pieces whole star anise
- 2 2- to 3-inch strips orange peel*
- 1 2- to 3-inch strip lemon peel*
  Apple wedges and/or star anise

In a 4- to 5-quart Dutch oven combine cider, cranberry juice, pomegranate juice, stick cinnamon, star anise, orange peel, and lemon peel. Bring to boiling; reduce heat. Simmer, covered, for 20 minutes. Using a slotted spoon, remove stick cinnamon, star anise, orange peel, and lemon peel. Pour the punch into 10 heatproof cups; garnish with apple and/or star anise. Makes 10 (8-ounce) servings.

*TEST KITCHEN TIP When removing orange and lemon peel from the fruit, avoid the white pith, which adds bitterness.

warm-me-ups

Mexicocoa Eggnog

✳

Start with ½ cup of tequila and taste before adding the additional ¼ cup. The amount to use depends on how much you like the distinct flavor of the spirit.

 3 cups dairy eggnog
 1 teaspoon ground nutmeg
 ½ teaspoon ground cloves
 ½ cup grated Mexican-style
   sweet chocolate, such
   as Ibarra
 4 to 6 ounces tequila (½ to ¾ cup)
   Mexican-style sweet
   chocolate shavings

In a large saucepan whisk together eggnog, nutmeg, and cloves until well combined. Heat mixture over low to medium-low heat until simmering (do not boil).

Slowly add the grated Mexican chocolate, whisking until the chocolate is melted. Remove from heat. Stir in tequila to combine.

Pour eggnog into four heatproof mugs. Sprinkle with Mexican chocolate shavings. Makes 4 (8-ounce) servings.

Peppermint Latte

✳

No espresso maker? Make espresso using instant espresso coffee powder.

 ½ cup prepared espresso coffee
 1 cup milk
 1 tablespoon crème de menthe
   syrup or peppermint schnapps
   Sugar (optional)
   Whipped cream
   Crushed peppermint candies or
   peppermint sticks

Prepare espresso according to machine manufacturer's directions.

Meanwhile, in a medium saucepan heat and stir milk until hot (do not boil). Stir in syrup or schnapps. Whisk

Caramel-Vanilla Cocoa

to froth. Divide the espresso between two heatproof cups.

Divide hot milk between the cups. If desired, sweeten to taste with sugar.

Spoon whipped cream into a pastry bag fitted with a large star tip. Pipe whipped cream on each serving; sprinkle with crushed peppermint candies or stir the beverage with a peppermint stick. Serve immediately. Makes 2 (6-ounce) servings.

Caramel-Vanilla Cocoa

✳

Stir in caramel ice cream topping to boost the richness of this hot cocoa.

 ½ cup sugar
 ½ cup unsweetened
   cocoa powder
 7 cups milk
 1 cup caramel-flavor
   ice cream topping
 1 teaspoon vanilla
   Marshmallows (optional)
   Caramel-flavor ice cream
   topping (optional)

In a large saucepan or 4-quart Dutch oven stir together sugar and cocoa powder until combined. Stir in ½ cup of the milk to form a smooth paste. Stir in remaining milk and the 1 cup ice cream topping. Stir over

medium heat just until heated through (do not boil). Remove from heat; stir in vanilla. Serve in eight heatproof cups. If desired, top with marshmallows and drizzle with additional topping. Makes 8 (about 8-ounce) servings.

Spiced-Buttered Rum Toddy

✳

Just as rich spices and brown sugar add fragrance to holiday baking, they add flavor to this warm toddy.

 3 tablespoons butter, softened
 3 tablespoons packed
   brown sugar
 ¼ teaspoon ground cloves
 ¼ teaspoon ground cinnamon
   Dash ground nutmeg
   Orange wedge
 ¼ cup turbinado sugar
 6 ounces amber rum, such as
   Mount Gay
 2 ounces Grand Marnier
 1½ cups boiling water
   Sweetened whipped cream
 4 cinnamon sticks

In a small mixing bowl beat butter and brown sugar with an electric mixer until combined. Add cloves, ground cinnamon, and nutmeg, beating to combine. Refrigerate overnight or until ready to use.

When ready to serve, moisten rims of four heatproof mugs with the orange wedge. Place the turbinado sugar in a saucer; slowly turn rims of mugs in sugar to coat.

Place 1 tablespoon of the butter-spice mixture in each sugar-rimmed mug. Add 1½ ounces rum and ½ ounce Grand Marnier to each mug. Divide boiling water evenly among mugs; stir to combine. Float a spoonful of whipped cream on top; garnish with a cinnamon stick. Makes 4 servings.

Spirits Savvy

Following are descriptions for some of the spirits called for in the recipes for this book.

Chambord: This liqueur is made from cognac and other spirits infused with black raspberries, honey, vanilla, and other berries. Sip on its own or add to sparkling wine for a refreshing aperitif.

Cognac: This French brandy hails from a region north of Bordeaux, in and around the town of Cognac. Choose young cognac (labeled VS for Very Special) for mixed drinks. Enjoy XO (Extra Old) cognac as an after-dinner drink. Sip VSOP (Very Superior Old Pale) cognac on its own or in cocktails.

Cointreau: A clear, colorless, brandy-based liqueur, Cointreau is infused with both sweet and bitter orange peels. Serve it straight or substitute it in drink recipes calling for triple sec.

Grand Marnier: Infused with bitter oranges and aged in oak casks, this amber-color, cognac-based liqueur is typically served at room temperature in a snifter.

Rum: Hailing primarily from the Caribbean, rum is made from sugarcane juice boiled to molasses, then fermented, distilled, and aged in oak. The drink in this chapter calls for amber rum, generally aged longer than white (clear) rum; amber rum brings a rich, warm flavor that's well suited to hot winter drinks.

107

Mexicocoa Eggnog,
Peppermint Latte

Enjoy Hanukkah amid royal hues of deep blue and pure white with lustrous gold accents.

dripping with gold

gilded Hanukkah tree

☙ Hang pairs of chocolate gelt and golden dreidels as ornaments from a stick-style tree.

What You'll Need...

- [ ] chocolate gelt coins
- [ ] blue ⅛-inch-wide satin ribbon
- [ ] glue dots
- [ ] blue ½-inch-wide blue sheer ribbon
- [ ] wood dreidels
- [ ] gold acrylic paint
- [ ] small paintbrush
- [ ] gold thread
- [ ] scissors
- [ ] 1½ yards each blue and gold 2-inch-wide wired ribbon
- [ ] decorative golden tree
- [ ] gold jewelry wire

1 For gelt ornaments, sandwich glue dots and both ends of a 6-inch length of satin ribbon between two gelt coins. Tie a 3-inch length of sheer craft ribbon in a knot around the satin ribbon loop at the base of the coin.

2 For dreidel ornaments, paint the dreidels with gold craft paint without painting over the Hebrew letters. When paint is dry, wrap the handle with a glue dot. Wrap the glue dot area with 6 inches of gold thread, beginning with the center of the length of thread. Wrap around the handle a few times until secure. Tie the thread at the ends to make a loop.

3 Embellish the tree with a large double bow made from blue and gold wired ribbons. Attach the bow to the tree with a short length of gold jewelry wire.

first-class dining

☙ Welcome guests with personalized place settings. Beaded napkin rings and elegant place cards enhance the gelt-sprinkled tablescape.

What You'll Need...

for napkin rings

- [ ] gold concave-shape napkin rings
- [ ] gold jewelry wire
- [ ] wire cutters
- [ ] faceted blue and gold beads in a variety of sizes

1 Cut jewelry wire long enough to wrap around the center of napkin ring plus 2 to 3 inches for overlap.

2 String beads on jewelry wire in a pattern.

3 Secure beads to napkin ring by twisting wire ends together. Trim excess wire and tuck ends into beads.

What You'll Need...

for place cards

- [ ] white cardstock
- [ ] scissors or crafts knife and cutting mat
- [ ] blue satin ribbon
- [ ] glue dots
- [ ] blue and gold faceted beads
- [ ] gold craft leaves
- [ ] blue pen
- [ ] small gold easels or plate holders

1 Cut white cardstock to a 2¼×3½-inch rectangle for each card.

2 Cut 3½-inch lengths of ribbon for each place card. Use glue dots to adhere ribbon ¼ inch from top edge of card.

3 Glue gold and blue beads and craft leaves to the card along blue ribbon. Write names on cards with blue ink.

4 Set place cards at place settings on small easels or plate holders.

forever fruit

Celebrate Kwanzaa
with the traditional feast
of fruits propped, stacked,
and tastefully decorated.

a pear for every place

For edible centerpieces, plant a pear at each place setting.
Rest pears in clear glass candleholders and tie berry picks to the
stems with flowing ribbon bows. For pears as decoration and not to
be eaten, display plastic or wax fruit.

zest for life

∾ Where to find the makings for a stunning Kwanzaa centerpiece? At the grocery store! Enhance the aroma in any room with a zesty fruit assortment. The zest, or outer rind, contains most of the pungent scent and rich color of citrus fruits. A few artful turns with a zester tool creates a fragrant spiral. (Brush zested lemons or limes with lemon juice to prevent browning.) This edible arrangement includes pears, apples, radishes, kumquats, and Brussels sprout rosettes —with sprigs of nonedible juniper.

celebrate with cheese

Enhance your holiday cooking and entertaining with three time-honored cheeses from England, France, and Spain.

the many choices of cheese

Gourmet cheeses from around the world are in markets everywhere, so take advantage! Serve three world-renowned favorites, England's Stilton, France's Comté, and Spain's Manchego, with fruit and bread. Or use them in holiday recipes in classic and all-new ways.

Stellar Stilton

Origin: Stilton gained attention in the 1700s, when travelers from London to York would stop for a rest at the Bell Inn, a coach house in Stilton that served a creamy blue-veined cheese. Although Stilton was never made in Stilton, the cheese eventually took its name from the town where so many travelers tasted it.

Today only a handful of dairies, all in the counties of Leicestershire, Nottinghamshire, and Derbyshire, are licensed to make England's beloved blue. Creamy and ivory hued, laced with blue veins throughout, the cheese is hailed for its rich and intense flavor.

On Its Own: This is a great blue to round out an appetizer cheese plate; it goes especially well with sweet fruits, such as grapes and pears.

In Recipes: Stilton crumbles well for salads and as a topper for soups; it also melts well in recipes.

Wine Pairing: Port with Stilton is a classic combination.

Good to Know: Slice Stilton (rather than crumble it) immediately after taking it out of the refrigerator—it slices best when it's cold.

113

Port-Baked Pears with Stilton,
recipe on page 114

Port-Baked Pears with Stilton

✳

Shown on page 113.

6 medium firm pears
½ cup port
½ cup walnut halves, toasted
6 ounces Stilton cheese,
    cut into 6 wedges
¼ cup honey

Preheat oven to 350°F. Core pears from the bottoms, leaving the stems intact. If necessary, trim bottoms of pears so they stand upright. Peel pears. Place pears in a 2-quart baking dish. Pour port over pears.

Bake, covered, for 15 minutes. Uncover dish and bake for 15 to 20 minutes more or until pears are tender, basting occasionally with the port in the baking dish. Cool slightly; spoon port over pears again.

Place warm pears, stem ends up, on serving dishes. Place walnut halves and cheese wedges alongside pears. Drizzle honey evenly over all. Serve warm. Makes 6 servings.

114

Silky Stilton Bisque

✳

This soup is light in body, so enjoy the bold, full flavors of Stilton without that "can't eat another bite" feeling.

⅓ cup butter
½ cup all-purpose flour
5 cups reduced-sodium
    chicken broth
1 12-ounce bottle unfiltered
    wheat beer
4 ounces Stilton cheese, crumbled
    (1 cup)
½ cup whipping cream
    Salt
    Freshly ground black pepper
    Croutons (optional)
1 recipe Caramelized Shallots
    (optional)

In a large saucepan melt butter over medium-low heat. Whisk in flour; cook and stir 1 to 2 minutes or until mixture is golden (do not brown). Whisk in the broth very slowly, taking care to keep the flour mixture smooth. Whisk in beer. Bring to simmering over medium heat; simmer, covered, for 15 minutes or until slightly thickened, whisking occasionally. Whisk in cheese until melted. Stir in whipping cream. Heat through. Season to taste with salt and pepper. If desired, top soup with croutons and shallots. Makes 8 servings.

CARAMELIZED SHALLOTS Cut 2 shallots into thin wedges. In a large skillet cook shallots in 2 tablespoons butter over medium heat for 5 to 7 minutes or until shallots are golden.

Fondue Comté

✳

If you've wondered what the fuss is about when it comes to fondue, try this version with French Comté or Gruyère. The right cheese makes all the difference.

1¼ pounds Comté cheese or
    Gruyère cheese, rind removed
    and cheese shredded (5 cups)
3 tablespoons all-purpose flour
1½ cups dry white wine
¼ cup milk
2 tablespoons dry sherry
⅛ teaspoon ground nutmeg
⅛ teaspoon ground white pepper
    Dippers, such as French bread
    cut into 1-inch cubes and
    toasted,* pretzel rods, apple
    slices, and/or pear slices

Bring shredded cheese to room temperature. Toss cheese with flour and set aside.

In a large saucepan heat wine over medium heat until small bubbles rise to the surface. Just before the wine boils, reduce heat to low and stir in the cheese mixture, a little at a time, stirring constantly and making sure cheese is melted before adding more cheese. Stir until the mixture bubbles gently.

Stir in milk, sherry, nutmeg, and pepper. Transfer cheese mixture to a fondue pot. Keep mixture bubbling gently over a fondue burner. Serve with dippers. If mixture becomes too thick, stir in a little warm milk. Makes 12 servings.

***TEST KITCHEN TIP** For toasted bread cubes, place cubes on a baking sheet. Place in a 350°F oven for 5 to 7 minutes or until crisp and toasted.

Silky Stilton Bisque

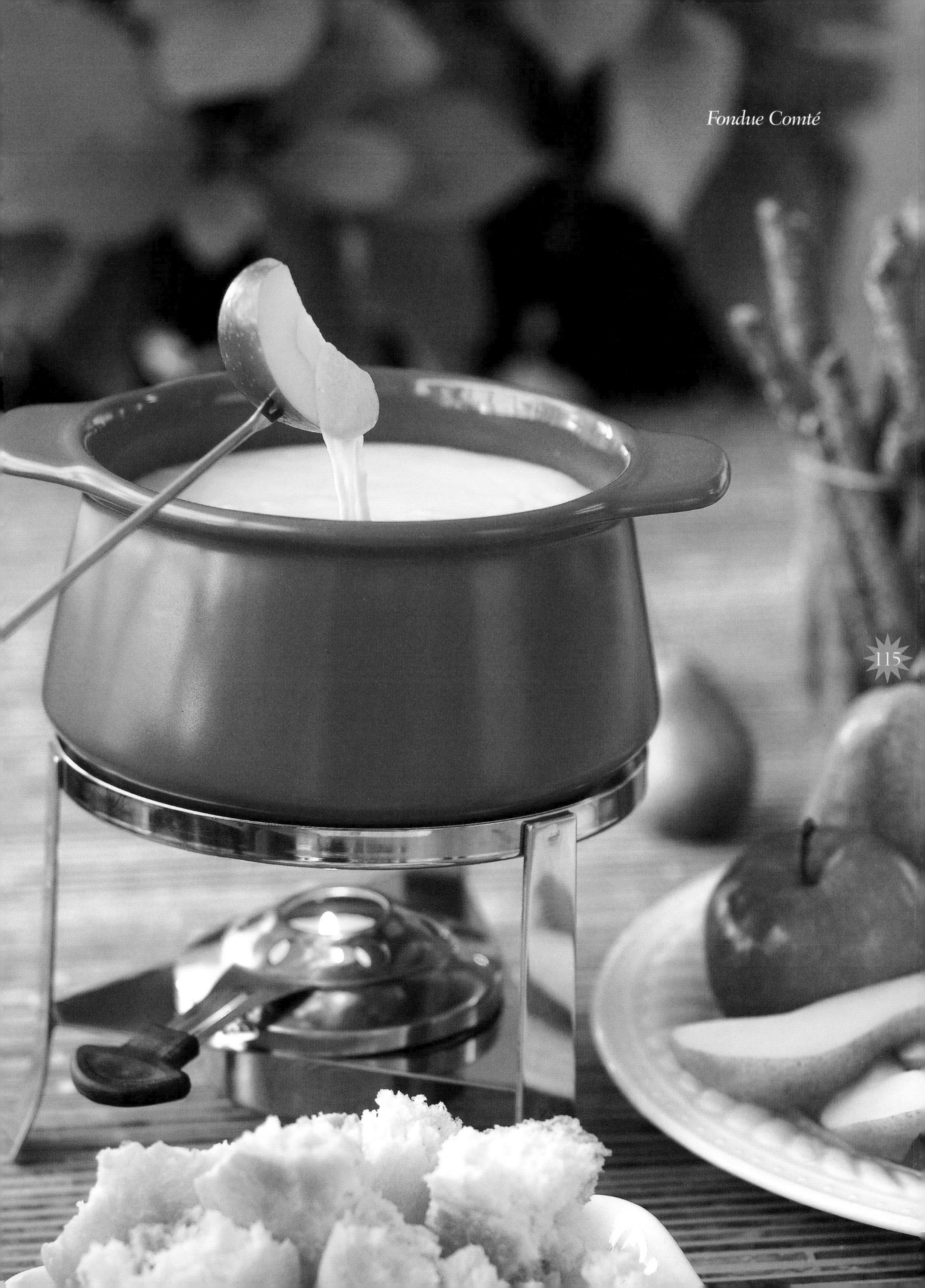

Fondue Comté

Chicken Comté-Curry Spread

Captivating Comté

Origin: Comté (kon-TAY) hails from France's rustic Jura Massif region, near Switzerland. It is made from the milk of the dappled Montbéliarde cows that graze on the flowered meadows of this lush mountainous terrain— pasturelands that add to the complex, varied flavors of the cheese.

Each 80-pound wheel of Comté ages 4 to 24 months, allowing its aromas and flavors to grow richer and deeper. While no two wheels of this artisanal cheese are exactly alike, they often exhibit fruit, caramel, nut, and even coffeelike notes.

On Its Own: Savor Comté solo to key in to its rich flavor. It also pairs nicely with walnuts and fresh or dried fruits as a cheese course.

In Recipes: Like its cousin, Swiss Gruyère, Comté melts beautifully in recipes, such as au gratin potatoes. It also melts nicely in sandwiches.

Wine Pairing: Aged cheeses go well with red wines, and Comté is no exception. White wine is traditional with fondue; try Soave or Pinot Grigio from Italy or Pinot Gris from Alsace, France.

Good to Know: Chefs in France have discovered that Comté complements the flavor of curry—try it in Chicken Comté-Curry Spread.

Chicken Comté-Curry Spread

✳

This spread is exceptional with baguette toasts, crackers, and sliced apples.

- ¼ cup dairy sour cream
- 3 tablespoons mayonnaise or salad dressing
- ¼ cup finely chopped toasted walnuts
- 2 tablespoons chopped green onion
- ¼ teaspoon curry powder
- ¼ teaspoon salt
- ⅛ teaspoon ground black pepper
- 1 cup shredded fresh spinach
- 2 ounces Comté cheese, cut into small matchstick pieces
- ½ cup finely chopped cooked chicken
  - Comté cheese, cut into small matchstick pieces (optional)

In a bowl combine sour cream and mayonnaise. Stir in walnuts, green onion, curry powder, salt, and pepper. Stir in spinach, the 2 ounces cheese, and chicken. Serve immediately or cover and refrigerate up to 2 hours. If desired, sprinkle with additional cheese. Makes 1⅔ cups.

Twice-Baked Potatoes with Comté Cheese

✳

This recipe rivals the all-out decadent twice-baked potatoes served at high-end steak houses. Comté cheese gives this version an edge.

- 4 large Yukon gold potatoes (about 2 pounds)
- 1 tablespoon olive oil
- 2 tablespoons butter
- ⅓ cup finely chopped shallots
- 1 tablespoon snipped fresh chives
- 1 tablespoon snipped fresh parsley
- 4 ounces Comté cheese or Gruyère cheese, shredded (1 cup)
- ⅓ cup snipped prosciutto (about 2 ounces)

- ¼ cup dairy sour cream
  - Milk
  - Salt and ground black pepper

Preheat oven to 400°F. Scrub potatoes thoroughly with a brush; pat dry. Rub potatoes with the oil. Wrap each potato in foil. Bake for 50 to 60 minutes or until tender. Discard foil. Let potatoes stand about 10 minutes to cool slightly. Cut potatoes in half lengthwise. Carefully scoop pulp out of each potato half, leaving a ¼- to ½-inch shell; set aside shells. Place potato pulp in a large bowl. Mash the potato pulp with a potato masher or electric mixer on low speed until nearly smooth.

In a small saucepan melt butter over medium heat; add shallots and cook until shallots are tender but not brown. Add chives and parsley; cook 30 seconds more. Add shallot mixture to mashed potatoes; beat until smooth. Stir in ¾ cup of the cheese, the prosciutto, and sour cream. If necessary, stir in a little milk to make desired consistency. Season to taste with salt and pepper. Mound potato mixture into reserved potato shells; sprinkle with remaining ¼ cup cheese. Place potatoes in a single layer in a 3-quart rectangular baking dish.

Bake, uncovered, about 20 minutes or until golden brown and heated through. Makes 8 servings.

MAKE-AHEAD DIRECTIONS
Prepare and stuff potato halves as directed. Place potatoes in a single layer in an airtight container. Cover and refrigerate up to 1 day. Place potatoes in a 3-quart rectangular baking dish. Bake, covered, in a 325°F oven for 30 minutes. Uncover and bake 15 minutes more or until potatoes are golden brown and heated through.

Manchego-Mushroom Quesadillas

✳

- 4 slices bacon, chopped
- ¼ cup chopped onion
- 1 clove garlic, minced
- 8 ounces portobello or button mushrooms, cut into bite-size pieces
- ¼ teaspoon crushed red pepper
- ¼ teaspoon Worcestershire sauce
- 2 tablespoons snipped fresh cilantro
- 1 tablespoon butter, cut into 4 pieces
- 4 ounces Manchego cheese or Monterey Jack cheese, shredded (1 cup)
- 4 7- or 8-inch flour tortillas
- ½ cup dairy sour cream
- ⅓ cup chopped tomato
- ⅓ cup chopped green sweet pepper
- 2 tablespoons sliced green onion

Preheat oven to 300°F. In a large skillet cook bacon over medium heat until bacon begins to crisp, stirring often. Add onion and garlic; cook and stir for 5 minutes or until onion is tender. Add mushrooms; cook and stir until tender. Remove from heat. Stir in crushed red pepper, Worcestershire, and cilantro.

In another large skillet or on a griddle melt one piece of the butter over medium heat. For quesadillas, sprinkle ¼ cup of the cheese over half of each tortilla. Top cheese with ⅓ cup of the mushroom mixture. Fold tortillas in half, pressing gently.

In prepared skillet cook one quesadilla for 2 to 3 minutes or until lightly browned; turn once. Remove from skillet; place on baking sheet. Keep warm in the oven. Repeat. Spoon sour cream into a bowl; sprinkle with tomato, sweet pepper, and green onion. Cut quesadillas into wedges; serve with sour cream mixture. Makes 4 appetizer servings.

Baked Eggs with Manchego

Baked Eggs with Manchego

✳

Why fuss with omelets when it's so easy to bake eggs to perfection? With a few well-chosen ingredients, the results are remarkable.

  2 tablespoons butter, softened
 12 eggs
 ¾ cup whipping cream
  3 ounces Manchego cheese, shredded (¾ cup)
    Freshly ground black pepper
  4 ounces pancetta, chopped, or 4 slices bacon, chopped (optional)
 ⅓ cup snipped fresh chives or parsley

Preheat oven to 350°F. Spread butter over the insides of six 10-ounce ramekins or baking dishes to coat. Arrange dishes on a 15×10×1-inch baking pan. Break 2 eggs into each dish; spoon 2 tablespoons cream over each and sprinkle each with 2 tablespoons cheese. Sprinkle each with pepper. Bake, uncovered, for 20 minutes or until yolks are nearly set.

Meanwhile, if desired, in a medium skillet cook pancetta or bacon over medium heat until browned and crisp, stirring occasionally. Using a slotted spoon, transfer pancetta to paper towels to drain.

To serve, sprinkle baked eggs with chives and, if desired, pancetta. Makes 6 servings.

*Greens with Manchego,
Serrano Ham, and Sherry Vinegar*

Greens with Manchego, Serrano Ham, and Sherry Vinegar

✳

Ingredients typical of the Mediterranean region—Serrano ham, Manchego cheese, sherry vinegar, and olive oil—star in this salad.

2 ounces Serrano ham or prosciutto, cut into 2×1-inch strips
1½ ounces Manchego cheese, cut into 1×¼-inch pieces
3 tablespoons olive oil
1 tablespoon sherry vinegar
1 clove garlic, minced
  Dash cayenne pepper
  Salt and ground black pepper
6 cups assorted salad greens

Wrap a strip of ham around each piece of cheese; set aside.

For dressing, in a small bowl whisk together oil, vinegar, garlic, and cayenne pepper. Season with salt and black pepper. Toss with greens; arrange on serving plates. Cut wrapped cheese pieces diagonally in half; arrange on greens. Makes 6 servings.

Marvelous Manchego

Origin: Manchego (mon-CHAY-go) is known as the "Cheese of Don Quixote." Both the cheese and the literary hero of the 17th-century novel hail from La Mancha—a fiercely rugged land on a high plateau in the interior of Spain.

True Manchego can be made only from whole milk of the hardy Manchega sheep that graze on the wheat and brush fields in this windy land of extreme temperatures. The resulting cheese—one of Spain's most famous—is mild, buttery, and nutty, with a hint of salty piquancy often found in other sheep's milk cheeses.

On Its Own: Manchego is often served as part of a tapas spread in Spanish taverns, where it's traditionally cut into thin (⅛-inch) triangles. Enjoy it as an appetizer with olives, bread, and cured meats. Also serve it as dessert with fresh fruits or cherry preserves.

In Recipes: Manchego slices and grates easily. Enjoy it with eggs, in salads, and paired with mushrooms.

Wine Pairing: Choose fruity reds, such as Spain's Rioja Crianza and France's Beaujolais wines. Spanish cava (sparkling wine) also meshes well with Manchego.

Good to Know: For these recipes, look for a younger Manchego rather than a long-aged version.

119

authentically speaking

For a cultural celebration of the Lunar New Year, prepare a lighthearted scene to ring out the old and ring in the new. Assemble lacquered dishes, paper fans, ornate chopsticks, coin-purse place card holders, and large and small Buddhas.

ring it in with takeouts

The spirit of the Chinese New Year rings true when sharing symbols of good fortune to start the year. Visit ethnic grocers and import stores to glean ideas and find worthy party decorations.

goodies to go

∿ Package fortune cookies dipped in melted white chocolate and sprinkled with colorful candies as party favors or dessert.

parting gifts

〜 Table decorations double as party favors: paper fans, chopsticks, and embroidered coin purses with place cards. Tuck candies in the purses for a sweet surprise.

front-door fortune

〜 Greet guests with a wish for the year ahead. Hang an ornament, such as a jade emblem for plenty, and attach a message mounted on gold and red cardstock.

clever carryout

〜 For gift giving or sharing leftovers, decorate take-out containers with metallic ribbon, coin beads, and jaunty tassels.

May 2009 be a plentiful year for you and your family.

123

Endive Scoops ▶

Belgian endive leaves are right-size scoops for luscious fillings. Try these combos:

■ A mixture of cream cheese, provolone, and goat cheese. Spread on endive; sprinkle with chopped figs and chopped pistachios.

■ Equal parts mascarpone cheese and purchased taramasalata (fish roe dip); top with capers and lemon peel shreds.

■ Softened cream cheese combined with chopped prosciutto, green onion, snipped fresh basil, and a dash of Worcestershire sauce. Spread on endive; sprinkle with chopped toasted pine nuts, finely shredded fontina cheese, and green onions.

In a Twinkling
no-recipe party bites

◀ **Dipped Strawberries**

Set out a few of these on a dessert buffet or as something sweet on the appetizer buffet. For best results, strawberries must be completely dry. Use paper towels to gently blot the berries before dipping. Sample these:

■ Melted milk chocolate, chopped salted cashews, pistachios, or mixed nuts.

■ Melted white chocolate on one side, dark chocolate on the other.

■ Dairy sour cream and brown sugar.

■ Buttery vanilla frosting and crunchy toasted coconut.

Deviled Eggs

Add these tasty tidbits to an egg yolk filling:

- Mexican sour cream dip, chopped chiles, chopped olives, and snipped cilantro.
- Confetti of finely chopped sweet peppers and ranch dressing. Sprinkle with thyme.
- Cooked bacon pieces and snipped fresh basil; garnish with sliced cherry tomatoes and shredded or snipped basil leaves.

▲ Sour Cream Dip

To basic sour cream dip, add stir-ins. For the dip, beat together one 8-ounce package softened cream cheese and one 8-ounce carton dairy sour cream with a mixer until fluffy. Stir in one of the following combinations:

- Chopped avocado, red onion, and garlic salt.
- Cooked and crumbled bacon, crumbled blue cheese, and finely chopped celery.

◄ Clever Canapés

Spread a small dab of butter on a canapé base to hold topping. Add:

- Sliced cucumber, smoked salmon, sour cream, and chives on crackers.
- Herbed cheese spread and cherry tomato wedge on fresh basil leaves.
- Horseradish spread, blue cheese, sliced roast beef, and green onion slices on melba toast or flatbread.

See "Family-Friendly Food Gifts", page 133.

126

GIVING
from the
HEART

Gather wrapping paper, bows, and gift tags. These clever handmade gifts will surprise all the special people in your life.

No last-minute trips to the mall here. These handsome gifts are thoughtfully personalized.

monogram magic

ties that bind

Purely masculine, this album is made to hold memories within while paying tribute to old favorites on the cover.

1 Open album out flat and measure both front and back covers. Allowing for ease to fit album into cover, add ½ inch to both top and bottom for seam allowances and approximately 8 inches to each side length for front and back flaps. From wool cut a piece this measurement. Press under and stitch a narrow hem along each flap end.

2 Place wool around closed album, centering, with excess fabric for flaps extending evenly. Position ties vertically on cover and trim even with upper edge of cover; baste in place at seam line.

3 Reposition wool (with basted ties in place) on album. Allowing for ease to fit, turn under wool to form flaps. Mark fold lines. Remove wool from album. Fold flaps right side facing cover and raw edges aligned; baste flaps along top and bottom seams.

4 Cut lining fabric the same measurement as wool cover with flaps basted in place. Right sides together, stitch lining to wool along top and bottom seam lines. Trim corners. Turn cover to right side; turn back flaps.

5 Slip album into cover. Glue neckties to wool cover. Attach letters to ties.

What You'll Need ...

- photo album, approximately 10x15 inches
- tape measure
- blue wool
- scissors
- iron
- sewing machine
- 3 neckties in coordinating colors
- ½ yard of 45-inch-wide cotton lining
- fabric glue
- 3 embroidered or fabric letters

good night

Personalize bed linens with monograms and coordinating ribbons.

What You'll Need ...

- sewing machine
- thread to match pillowcase
- embroidery feature pillowcases
- 1½ yards each of 2 ribbon trims in ⅝- to 1-inch widths

1 Machine-embroider monograms on pillowcases.

2 Trim pillowcase with ribbons by machine-topstitching along the hemmed edge.

map manager

 Just the right size to hold maps, this handy customized organizer begins with a place mat.

1 Fold over one-third of a place mat to form a pocket large enough to hold maps.

2 Mark button placement on each side of pocket, close to the edge.

3 Sew buttons as marked, sewing through both layers of the place mat. Knot firmly on the back side.

4 Glue strips of coordinating ribbon to wrap around inside and outside of fold-over flap. Glue on wooden initial letters using wood glue.

What You'll Need...

- craft glue for metal
- wooden rectangular box with frame lid
- metal sheet to fit inside lid frame
- decorative scrapbook papers cut to fit lid frame
- assorted alphabet magnets or scrapbook alphabets and magnetic strips

trinket box

🐚 Alphabet magnets are movable and interchangeable on a box lid with a metal insert.

1 Glue metal sheet to box lid frame.

2 Insert decorative scrapbook paper into the frame; close the back.

3 Arrange magnetic alphabet in a monogram on the lid.

family-friendly food gifts

Fun to make and delightful to give, these yummy sweets and snacks are packaged to guarantee smiles.

When Giving Food Gifts …

To ensure that food gifts are appreciated to the fullest:
- Always package foods in food-safe containers.
- Label gifts with contents and how to prepare and/or serve.
- List storage instructions along with a date by which the food should be consumed.

Cocoa Tassies with Peppermint Filling

✳

Combine luscious chocolate, airy marshmallow crème, and peppermint for a trio of flavor.

- 1¼ cups all-purpose flour
- ⅓ cup sugar
- ¼ cup unsweetened cocoa powder
- ½ cup cold butter
- 1 egg yolk, lightly beaten
- 2 tablespoons cold water
- 1 recipe Peppermint Cream Filling Striped round peppermint candies

For cocoa shells, in a medium bowl stir together flour, sugar, and cocoa powder. Using a pastry blender, cut in butter until mixture is crumbly. In a small bowl combine egg yolk and water. Gradually stir egg yolk mixture into flour mixture. Gently knead dough just until a ball forms. If necessary, cover dough with plastic wrap; refrigerate for 30 to 60 minutes or until dough is easy to handle. **Preheat oven to 375°F.** Divide dough into 36 pieces. Press dough pieces onto bottoms and up sides of 1¾-inch muffin cups. Bake for 8 to 10 minutes or until shells are firm. Cool in muffin cups for 5 minutes. Remove shells from muffin cups. Cool completely.

For filling, prepare Peppermint Cream Filling. Using a pastry bag fitted with an open star tip, pipe filling into the cocoa shells. Top with peppermint candies. Enjoy filled tassies within 2 hours. Makes 36.

PEPPERMINT CREAM FILLING In a large mixing bowl combine ¼ cup butter, softened; one 7-ounce jar marshmallow crème; and ½ teaspoon peppermint extract. Beat with an electric mixer on medium speed until smooth. Gradually beat in 1½ cups powdered sugar. Beat in 1 tablespoon milk. Beat in 1 cup powdered sugar. Using a wooden spoon, stir in 1 cup powdered sugar. If necessary, stir in enough additional milk, 1 teaspoon at a time, to make filling of piping consistency.

TO STORE Place unfilled shells in layers separated by waxed paper in an airtight container; cover. Store at room temperature up to 3 days or freeze up to 3 months. Thaw shells, if frozen. Fill as directed above.

TO PRESENT AS SHOWN Mark every ½ inch around the border of a square paper plate. Paper-punch where marked. Beginning at one corner, lace ribbon through the holes. Tie a bow with the ribbon ends, adding a jingle bell and chenille-stem spirals.

Cocoa Tassies with Peppermint Filling

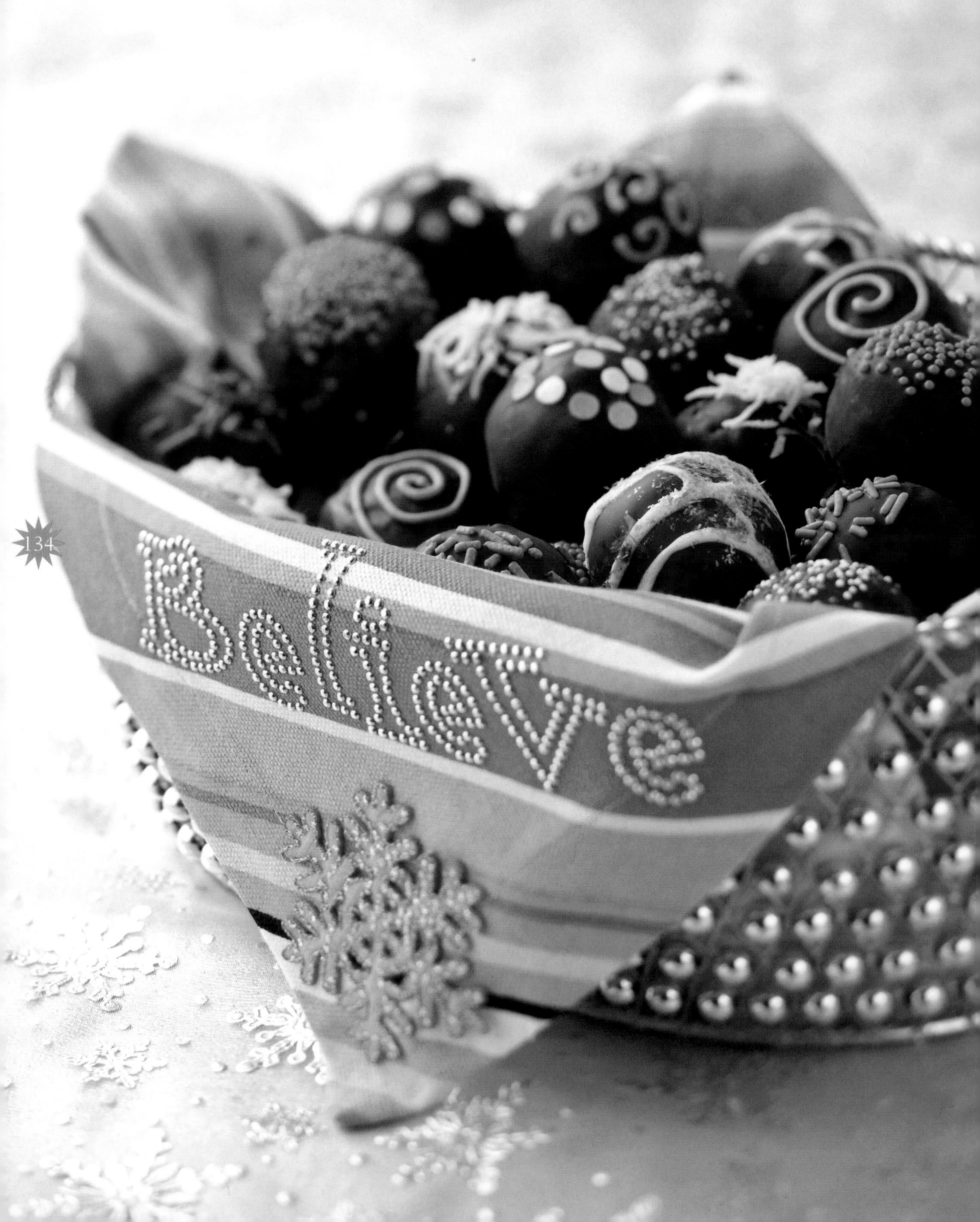
Believe

Doughnut Delights

✳

Surprise and delight an entire family with a container of decorated doughnuts to enjoy while opening presents.

1½ cups bittersweet chocolate pieces
1 tablespoon shortening
1 teaspoon ground cinnamon
24 glazed doughnut holes
Shredded coconut, assorted sprinkles, nonpareils, and/or edible glitter
1 recipe Powdered Sugar Icing (optional)

In a medium microwave-safe bowl place chocolate pieces and shortening. Microwave on 50 percent power (medium) for 1 to 2 minutes or until chocolate is melted and smooth, stirring after each minute. Stir in cinnamon.

Arrange doughnut holes on a tray or baking sheet lined with waxed paper. Spoon chocolate over each doughnut hole and sprinkle with coconut, sprinkles, nonpareils, and/or edible glitter. Let stand about 30 minutes or until set. If desired, drizzle or pipe Powdered Sugar Icing on chocolate-covered balls. Makes 24 doughnut holes.

POWDERED SUGAR ICING
In a small bowl combine 1 cup powdered sugar, 1 tablespoon milk, and ¼ teaspoon vanilla. Stir in additional milk, 1 teaspoon at a time, until icing is of piping or drizzling consistency. If desired, tint icing with food coloring.

TO PRESENT AS SHOWN
Trim the corner of a cloth napkin with a pretty iron-on message and snowflake, following manufacturer's directions for bonding.

Double-Chocolate Spiced Snack Mix

Double-Chocolate Spiced Snack Mix

✳

Gift recipients will love snack mixes that keep up to one week.

1 12-ounce package crispy corn and rice cereal (about 10 cups)
1½ cups mixed nuts
½ cup packed brown sugar
½ cup light-color corn syrup
½ cup butter
1 teaspoon ground cinnamon
½ teaspoon ground ginger
1½ cups chocolate-covered peanuts or chocolate-covered raisins
1½ cups bittersweet, semisweet, or milk chocolate pieces

Preheat oven to 300°F. In a large roasting pan combine cereal and nuts; set aside.

In a small saucepan combine brown sugar, corn syrup, butter, cinnamon, and ginger. Cook and stir over medium heat until butter is melted and mixture is smooth. Pour over cereal mixture; stir gently to coat.

Bake for 30 minutes, stirring twice. Remove from oven. Spread mixture onto a large piece of buttered foil and let cool. Break into pieces and place in a bowl. Stir in chocolate-covered peanuts or raisins and chocolate pieces. Place in an airtight container. Makes 16 cups.

TO STORE Cover and store in an airtight container at room temperature up to 1 week.

TO PRESENT AS SHOWN
Paint a wood ball knob with red acrylic paint; let dry. Dip a pencil eraser in white acrylic paint and dot onto the knob; let dry. Wearing safety glasses, drill a hole in the lid of a metal container. Attach the knob using a short screw.

135

Marshmallow Truffles

Marshmallow Truffles

✳

Elegant on the outside and sweet throughout, these pretty candies delight all ages.

    1   7-ounce jar marshmallow crème
    ⅓   cup butter, softened
    ¼   teaspoon almond extract
          or vanilla
    ¼   teaspoon salt
    3   cups powdered sugar
          Powdered sugar
          Toasted whole almonds,
            toasted pecan halves, toasted
            macadamia nuts, toasted
            hazelnuts (filberts), quartered
            pitted dates, and/or
            dried cherries
    8   ounces white baking chocolate,
            chopped*
    1   tablespoon shortening
          Coarse green sugar, finely
            chopped toasted nuts, toasted
            coconut, or candy sprinkles
          White baking chocolate, melted
          Red paste food coloring

Line a large baking sheet with waxed paper; butter the paper. Set aside. In a large mixing bowl combine marshmallow crème, butter, almond extract, and salt. Beat with an electric mixer until smooth. Gradually add the 3 cups powdered sugar, beating until well mixed. Cover and refrigerate about 1 hour or until mixture is easy to handle.

Lightly dust your hands with additional powdered sugar; shape marshmallow mixture into 1-inch balls, forming the mixture around a whole almond, pecan half, macadamia nut, hazelnut, date piece, or dried cherry (you may need more marshmallow mixture to completely cover pecan halves and almonds). Place balls on prepared baking sheet. Cover lightly; freeze for 20 minutes.

Meanwhile, in a small saucepan combine 8 ounces white chocolate and shortening. Heat and stir over low heat until melted and smooth. Remove from heat.

Line another large baking sheet with waxed paper; set aside. Remove balls, a few at a time, from the freezer. Dip balls in chocolate. Use a fork to gently lift balls out of chocolate, drawing the fork across the rim of the saucepan to remove excess chocolate. Place balls on the prepared baking sheet. Immediately sprinkle tops with coarse green sugar, finely chopped nuts, toasted coconut, or candy sprinkles. Let stand at room temperature about 15 minutes or until completely set. Tint some melted chocolate with red paste food coloring. Drizzle truffles with tinted chocolate. Refrigerate. Makes about 40 truffles.

*TEST KITCHEN TIP Use 8 ounces vanilla-flavor candy coating instead of (or in addition to) the white baking chocolate. If using both candy coating and baking chocolate, in separate small saucepans combine candy coating or white baking chocolate with 1 tablespoon shortening; melt, dip, and decorate truffles as directed. (There will be leftover melted candy coating and chocolate, but use 8 ounces of each for enough depth to dip truffles.)

TO STORE Place truffles in layers separated by waxed paper in an airtight container; cover. Store in the refrigerator up to 1 week or freeze up to 3 months.

TO PRESENT AS SHOWN Using a clear glass plate as a guide for size, cut two slightly different-size circles from coordinating scrapbook papers. Attach circles together using double-sided tape. Center and tape circles to the bottom of the clear plate or nest them between a pair of plates.

Fruit-and-Nut Cheese Balls

Fruit-and-Nut Cheese Balls

✳

A hit with children.

    2   8-ounce packages cream cheese,
          softened
    1   8-ounce can crushed pineapple
          (juice pack), well drained
    2   3.75-ounce packages honey
          roasted-flavor sliced almonds
          or 1½ cups honey roasted-
          flavor whole almonds, coarsely
          chopped
    ⅔   cup dried cranberries
    ½   cup finely chopped green onions
    1   teaspoon seasoned salt
    3   drops bottled hot pepper sauce
          Assorted crackers

In a large mixing bowl beat cream cheese with an electric mixer until fluffy. Beat in pineapple, one package of the almonds, dried cranberries, ¼ cup of the green onions, seasoned salt, and hot pepper sauce. Cover; refrigerate for 4 to 24 hours.

Shape cheese mixture into two balls; roll each ball in remaining nuts and remaining green onions. Let stand for 15 minutes. Serve with crackers. Makes about 3⅓ cups.

TO STORE Cover and refrigerate any remaining cheese up to 24 hours.

TO PRESENT AS SHOWN Tie a large ribbon bow around the stem of a pedestal bowl.

137

Marshmallow Snowmen

✳

Unabashedly sweet, these portly pals appear to hail from a snowy front yard. Create them with your kids for an afternoon of fun.

- 12 vanilla caramels, unwrapped (¼ of a 14-ounce package)
- 3 tablespoons sweetened condensed milk
- 2 tablespoons butter
- 1 10-ounce package large marshmallows (about 39) Marshmallow crème
- 53 pretzel sticks
- 1 cup chopped pistachio nuts, coconut, toffee pieces, and/or ⅓ cup nonpareils
- 4 ounces bittersweet, semisweet, or milk chocolate pieces
- 2 teaspoons shortening Miniature candy-coated semisweet chocolate pieces, tiny round candies, strawberry- or cherry-flavor rolled fruit leather, fruit-flavor ring-shape jelly candies, and miniature pretzel twists

Line a large baking sheet with foil; butter the foil. Set aside. In a small saucepan combine caramels, sweetened condensed milk, and butter. Heat and stir over medium-low heat until melted and smooth.

Using kitchen scissors, cut one-third of the marshmallows in half crosswise.* Place each marshmallow half, sticky side down, on top of a whole marshmallow. Press together gently to seal. If necessary, spread a small amount of marshmallow crème between the marshmallow pieces to hold them together. For arms, insert pretzel sticks into opposite sides of each whole marshmallow.

Marshmallow Snowmen

Dip bottom one-third of each marshmallow stack into melted caramel mixture. Allow excess to drip off. Place dipped marshmallows on prepared baking sheet.

Place pistachio nuts, coconut, toffee pieces, and/or nonpareils in separate small bowls.

In another small saucepan combine chocolate pieces and shortening. Stir over low heat until melted and smooth.

Dip each caramel-coated marshmallow stack in melted chocolate, covering bottom of stack with chocolate. Allow excess to drip off. Immediately dip chocolate-covered marshmallow in nuts, coconut, toffee pieces, and/or nonpareils. Return stack to baking sheet. Let stand about 30 minutes or until chocolate sets.

Remelt chocolate in saucepan over low heat, if necessary. Place snowmen flat. To make eyes and buttons, dip one end of a pretzel stick into melted chocolate; dab chocolate onto marshmallows. For a nose, dab on chocolate and attach a small round candy. Let stand about 5 minutes or until set. For a hat, shape a rolled fruit leather; attach with a small amount of marshmallow crème. For earmuffs, place fruit ring candy between waxed paper. With a rolling pin, slightly flatten fruit ring;

½ cup finely chopped, drained
    maraschino cherries
¼ teaspoon almond extract
60 vanilla wafers
12 ounces chocolate-flavor candy
    coating, coarsely chopped
2 teaspoons shortening
4 ounces vanilla-flavor candy
    coating, coarsely chopped
1 teaspoon shortening

For filling, in a medium mixing bowl beat cream cheese and powdered sugar with an electric mixer on medium speed until combined. Stir in cherries and almond extract with a wooden spoon. Spread filling on the flat sides of half the cookies. Top with remaining cookies, flat sides down. Cover and refrigerate about 30 minutes or until filling is firm.

In a small saucepan melt chocolate-flavor candy coating and the 2 teaspoons shortening over low heat. Remove from heat. Using a fork, dip each cookie into the chocolate to completely cover. Allow excess to drip off. Place cookies on waxed paper until chocolate sets (about 30 minutes).

In another small saucepan melt vanilla-flavor candy coating and the 1 teaspoon shortening over low heat; cool. Spoon into a resealable plastic bag; seal bag. Snip off a tiny corner of the bag. Drizzle candy coating over dipped cookies in a tree design. Set aside until set. Refrigerate. Makes 30 cookies.

TO STORE Place cookies in layers separated by waxed paper in an airtight container; cover. Store in the refrigerator up to 3 days. Do not freeze the cookies.

TO PRESENT AS SHOWN Hot-glue feather trim around the rim of a small basket. Using ribbon, tie on a pair of coordinating ornaments. Stack cookies in a cellophane bag and tie with a ribbon.

139

Chocolate-Cherry Dips

roll in sugar. Attach with a small amount of marshmallow crème. Use a small piece of fruit leather for a strap and a strip of fruit leather for a scarf, securing with marshmallow crème. For antlers, snip marshmallow "head" with kitchen shears. Insert miniature pretzel twists in the marshmallow slits using a small amount of marshmallow crème. Place in paper candy cups. Makes about 26.

TO STORE Layer snowmen between pieces of waxed paper in an airtight container. Cover and store at room temperature up to 3 days.

*TEST KITCHEN TIP Coat kitchen scissors with nonstick cooking

spray or dip into hot water to cut marshmallows.

TO PRESENT AS SHOWN Trim a clear glass platter with rub-on vellum stickers. Because the snowmen sit in papers, you can put stickers on the entire plate, but don't let them come in direct contact with the food.

Chocolate-Cherry Dips

With fancy two-chocolate coating, these cuties are satisfyingly sweet.

½ of an 8-ounce package cream
    cheese, softened
½ cup powdered sugar

what a trip

For travelers, give gifts that keep belongings together and easily identified.

funky flower tote

With bright felt, whimsical stitches, and a bold design, this classy tote blooms. Crafted in a pyramid shape, the carryall is a roomy travel companion.

1 Trace pattern pieces on **pages 156–157**. Use the patterns to cut the corresponding pieces from felt, with pinking shears if desired. In addition, cut the following:

11 – 1⅛-inch pinked felt circles from purple
11 – ⅞-inch felt circles from teal
1 – 1¾-inch pinked felt circle from purple
1 – 1½-inch felt circle from teal

2 Piece front design according to diagram on **page 156**, layering felt. Press; topstitch on fold lines of bottom and flap as indicated.

3 Using the photo as a guide, trace floral design pieces onto fusible webbing. Fuse floral design pieces to corresponding felt. Cut out. Arrange design on bag front; fuse according to manufacture's instructions.

4 Machine-topstitch in place with matching threads. Using photo as a guide, embroider the floral design with straight stitches, stem stitches, French knots, fly stitches, and lazy daisy stitches as shown on **page 157**.

5 Cut and layer felt circles according to photo. Secure circles to bag front and flap using straight stitches and a French knot in center.

6 Match points on side boxing and handle to letters on bag. Place front and back pieces with raw sides together. Topstitch together ¼ inch from edge. Sew on snap closure.

unmistakably yours

One-of-a-kind luggage tags are helpful in locating bags at a glance. Print a message or word in a funky font. Back it with colorful scrapbook papers. Get the tag laminated at a print or office supply shop. Add an eyelet and chain for these mini messengers to attach to suitcase handles, securing the clasp with pliers if necessary. On the opposite side, leave room for name and address labels.

countdown to Christmas

let it snow · let it snow

NOEL

Sing a
carol to
grandpa

So many uses, so many ways to delight with tiny boxes of big surprises.

little boxes

Use boxes for each day of Advent or as gift containers. The mini wonders capture curiosities.

What You'll Need...

- [ ] round papier-mâché boxes with lids
- [ ] scrapbook papers
- [ ] scissors; pencil
- [ ] glue stick
- [ ] silver cord
- [ ] hot-glue gun and glue sticks
- [ ] assorted trims, such as ribbon, jingle bells, small ornaments, candy canes, alphabet trims, and miniature trees and flowers

1. Cut paper strips to fit box and lid rims. Trace the lid onto paper; cut out circle. Use glue stick to adhere paper pieces to box. If the lid fits the box snuggly, trim the box paper to fit just below where the lid rests.

2. Hot-glue cord around the edge of the lid. Hot-glue trims to the lid.

Tiny boxes can hold a multitude of fun surprises.

Here is a treasure of tuck-inside items sure to make unforgettable holiday memories.

Handwritten notes:
- "Sleep by the Christmas tree."
- "Call Grandma and Grandpa and sing them a carol."
- "Good for a batch of your favorite cookies."
- "You can stay up an extra hour tonight."
- "Let's watch a new holiday DVD together."
- "Good for a cup of hot chocolate and popcorn."

Small gifts:
- Holiday ornament
- Wrapped candies
- Jewelry
- Coins or rolled-up bills
- Photograph
- Gift card
- Travel-size lotion
- Nail polish
- Toys, such as cars, dolls, or animals

143

▶ **Merry Markers** When the gang's all present, personalize each glass with a pretty tie-on. Press an adhesive initial on a vellum tag and thread on cording with metal charms from scrapbook supplies. If desired, use glue dots to tack the trims in place.

In a Twinkling
eat, drink & be merry

▲ **On the Curve** Create holiday cheer napkin rings using pliable metal stickers available with scrapbooking supplies. Simply remove the paper backing and shape the stickers around matching rings.

◀ **Sprinkle and Dash** Add polka dots to salt and pepper shakers. Dip a pencil eraser or tip into glass paint and dot onto surface.

▼ **Recipe Exchange** Share holiday cookie recipes with friends and family. Fold over a piece of paper and trace a cookie cutter shape along the fold. Use marking pens to draw details on the front and jot down a recipe inside.

▲ **Beaded Beauties** Serving utensils and cloth napkins glint elegance when dressed in spangles. To wrap the utensils, string beads on fine wire and wrap around the handles. Use embroidery floss to stitch beads in a floral pattern to the corner of a napkin.

◀ **Gadget Heaven** Christmas oven mitts do double duty as gift holders. Stuff the mitts with oodles of kitchen gadgets to surprise the cooks on your list.

See "What a Dish", pages 150–151

JUST *for* KIDS

Hours of giggly fun are in store
when eager kids gather at
the table with an array of bright
crafting supplies.

oodles of noodles

Shop the pasta and specialty foods aisles for noodles in all sorts of shapes and sizes. Then watch the kids craft clever ornaments and designs pretty enough to frame.

picture pasta

Fun to give as gifts or to personalize your room, these artsy framed pieces are a blast to make.

What You'll Need...

- simple flat frames
- cardboard trimmed to fit inside frame or the frame backing board
- pencil
- assorted pasta
- white glue
- paper plate
- small round paintbrush
- toothpick
- acrylic paints

1 Place trimmed cardboard or frame backing board into the frame and draw a line on the cardboard along the inside edge of the frame to serve as an outline for the design. Do not put pasta outside the line.

2 Plan a design to make on the board. Arrange pasta of different sizes to make flowers, butterflies, bugs, hearts, animals, or any other design.

3 Squirt a quarter-size dab of white glue on a paper plate. Use a paintbrush or toothpick to apply glue, either on the board or the back of the pasta. Place the pasta to create art. Let it dry. Rinse brush thoroughly and let dry.

4 Paint the background color first. For a design like the pink flower art, paint the entire piece purple, including the flower, leaves, and stars. Let it dry.

5 Paint the next layer of color over the purple. Use very little paint on a brush to apply over the purple. To allow the purple shadowing to show in the deep ridges, brush the pasta lightly. Don't allow the paint to be too thick or to run down into the background and cracks. Paint the flower pink, the leaves green, and tiny flowers yellow. Let dry.

6 Make the frame in the same manner. Cover the entire front and sides if you wish with pasta. Let dry.

7 Paint the whole frame one color, such as teal green. Use a paintbrush to get into all the tiny cracks. Let dry.

8 Choose another color, such as lime green, to go on top. Again use very little paint on the brush, just enough to cover the top edges of the pasta. Let dry.

9 Insert pasta art into the frame.

textured trims

Familiar cookie shapes trimmed with pasta are great for hanging on the tree or giving to grandparents.

1 Trace an ornament pattern from page 158. Cut out the shape. Draw around the shape on two pieces of cardboard; cut out.

2 On a baking sheet lined with waxed paper, brush one cardboard cutout with wood glue. Sprinkle on pasta to cover, as shown in **Photo A**. Let glue dry.

3 Paint the entire pasta-covered shape black if making the gingerbread boy (**Photo B**) or tree. Paint blue for the snowman. Paint the snowman hat black. Let dry.

4 Use very little paint on a brush to apply over the base color. Use brown for the gingerbread boy (**Photo C**), green for the tree, white for the snowman body, and blue for the hat. To allow background color to show in the ridges, brush the pasta lightly, keeping the paint from being too thick or running into the background and cracks. Let dry.

5 Paint the ornament details, such as tree trims, faces, gingerbread man outline, and buttons as shown in **Photo D**. Let the paint dry.

6 Make a hanging loop from cord and hot-glue to the ornament back. Hot-glue the remaining cardboard shape to the back. Paint if desired. Let dry.

7 Tie ribbon around the neck of the gingerbread boy or snowman.

149

A

B

C

D

what a dish

Snack time

will be even brighter
with these colorful
dishes on the table.

pattern-play dinnerware

Use colorful tissue paper to make designer-style dishes. They're perfect for playing house or enjoying a cookie and milk after school.

151

1 Tear, cut, or punch out tissue paper in a variety of small shapes, including strips.

2 If desired, punch the tissue paper for interest when layering colors.

3 Following the directions on the label of the decoupage medium, adhere the paper to the back sides of dishes. Let the decoupage medium dry.

NOTE Do not immerse the tissue paper-covered dishes in water. Wash the unpapered side with soapy water and rinse carefully, trying to avoid getting the paper side wet.

door decor

Put a personal stamp on your bedroom with a supercool name plaque. You just might want to make one for your very best friend too!

fishing plaque

Young anglers will love this name plate hanging on the bedroom door.

1 Nail a picture hanger to the back of the mounting piece, centered and slightly toward the top.

2 Cut a 36-inch length of each floss color; knot the ends together. Wrap the first letter with floss and hot-glue it in place toward the top of the backing wood. Continue wrapping and gluing letters to the background, using a bobber in place of an "o" if desired. Small bobbers also can be used to dot an "i."

3 Arrange the lures and remaining floss below the name and hot-glue in place.

princess plaque

For girly girls of all ages, this magical wall art is crafted from premade letters and party favor accents.

1 Plan arrangement of letters, favors, and colors on the wooden plate.

2 Lay out newspapers. Put a quarter-size dab of acrylic paints onto paper plate.

3 Paint the wooden plate on one side first and let it dry. Paint the other side. Paint the letter. Let dry. Apply second coats if necessary. Let dry.

4 Put a quarter-size dab of adhesive onto the paper plate. Use a toothpick to put pea-size dabs of adhesive on the back side of the letter only where it will touch the wooden plate.

5 If the tiara has teeth on the comb section, ask an adult to carefully break off the teeth of the comb using pliers. This will help you place it onto the project more easily. Use the adhesive to attach the tiara, wand, and remaining letters on the wooden plate. Let adhesive dry.

6 Adhere a stick-on hanger to the back of the wooden plate center, toward the top.

project details

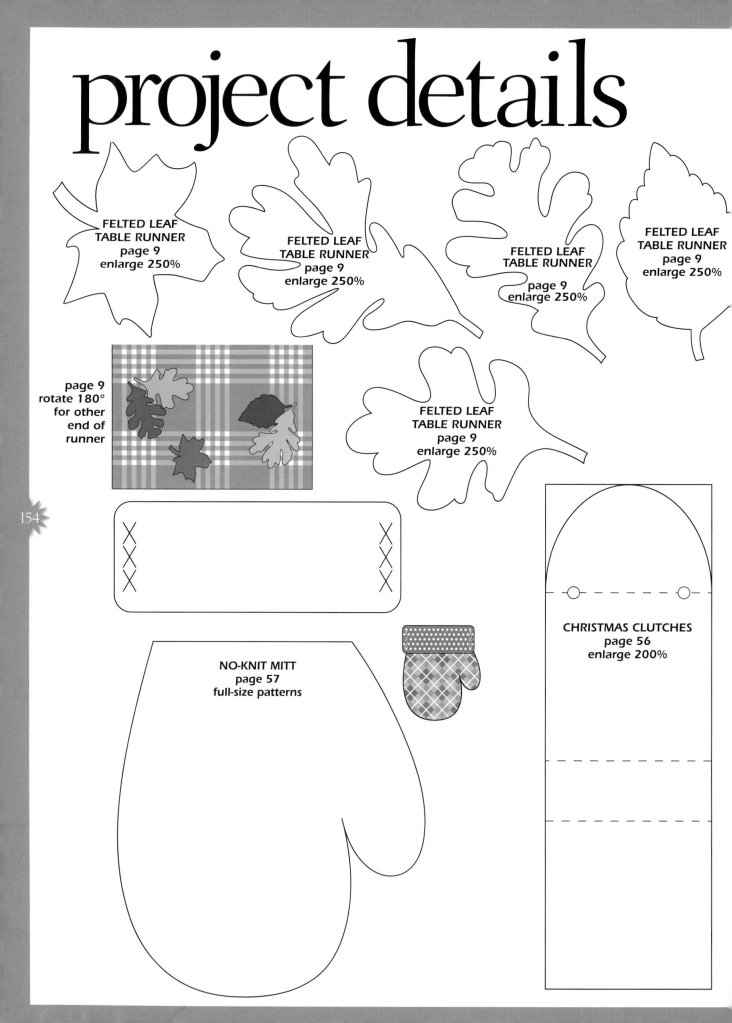

FELTED LEAF
TABLE RUNNER
page 9
enlarge 250%

FELTED LEAF
TABLE RUNNER
page 9
enlarge 250%

FELTED LEAF
TABLE RUNNER
page 9
enlarge 250%

FELTED LEAF
TABLE RUNNER
page 9
enlarge 250%

page 9
rotate 180°
for other
end of
runner

FELTED LEAF
TABLE RUNNER
page 9
enlarge 250%

154

NO-KNIT MITT
page 57
full-size patterns

CHRISTMAS CLUTCHES
page 56
enlarge 200%

FALLING SNOWFLAKES
THROW
pages 82–83
enlarge 250%

KNIT WHIT STOCKINGS
pages 80–81
enlarge 250%
cut 1 sweater front,
2 felt pieces,
and 1 fusible web

FALLING SNOWFLAKES
THROW
pages 82–83
enlarge 250%

WINTER WOOL
PLACE MAT
pages 46–47
enlarge 125%

155

project details *continued*

**FUNKY FLOWER
TOTE FLAP LINING**
cut 1 from blue felt

FUNKY FLOWER TOTE
pages 140–141
enlarge
all patterns
400%

Fold here for front and back flap

● A   A ●

**FUNKY FLOWER TOTE
FRONT AND BACK**
cut 1 on fold from purple felt

Fold

● A   A ●

**FUNKY
FLOWER
TOTE
HANDLE
AND
SIDE BOXING**
cut 1
on fold from
purple felt,
cut 1
slightly larger
from blue felt

● B   Fold here for bottom boxing   B ●

Fold

● B   B ●

**FUNKY FLOWER TOTE
PLACEMENT DIAGRAM**

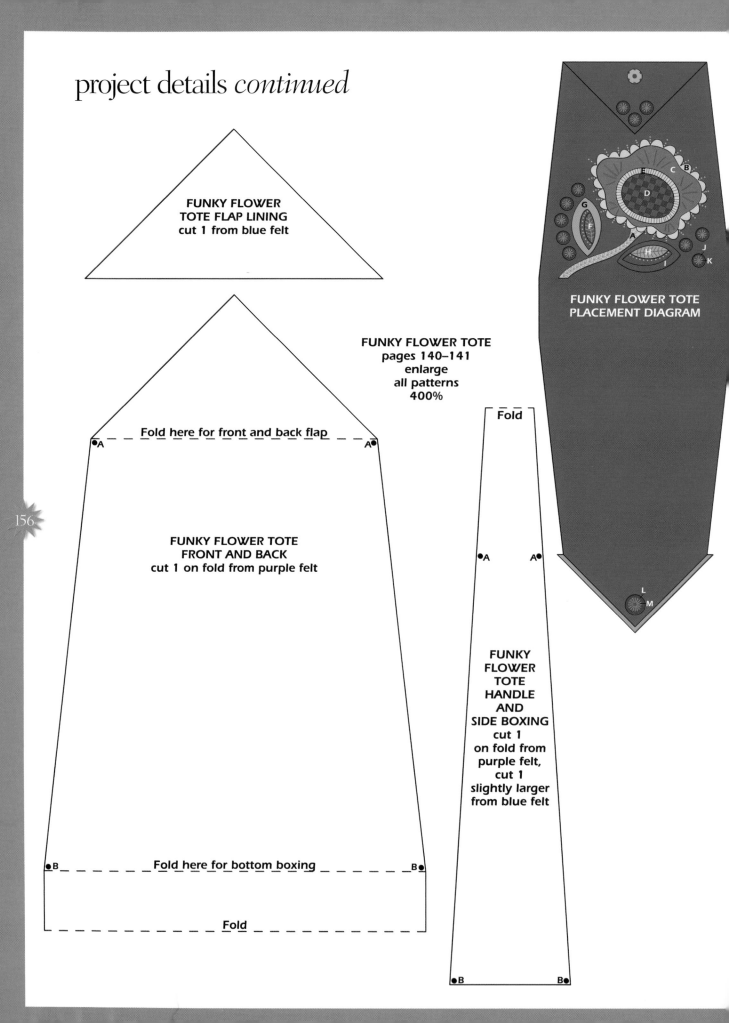

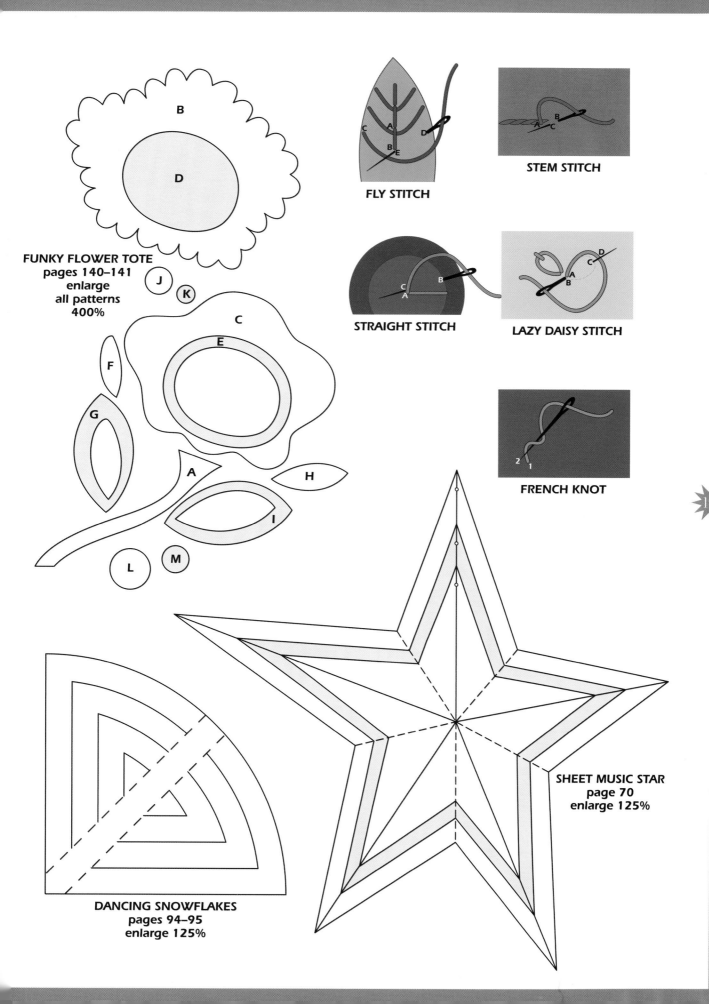

FUNKY FLOWER TOTE
pages 140–141
enlarge
all patterns
400%

B

D

J

K

C

E

F

G

A

H

I

L

M

FLY STITCH

STEM STITCH

STRAIGHT STITCH

LAZY DAISY STITCH

FRENCH KNOT

2 1

DANCING SNOWFLAKES
pages 94–95
enlarge 125%

SHEET MUSIC STAR
page 70
enlarge 125%

project details *continued*

**TEXTURED TRIMS
GINGERBREAD BOY**
page 149
full-size pattern

**TEXTURED TRIMS
SNOWMAN**
page 149
full-size pattern

**TEXTURED TRIMS
TREE**
page 149
full-size pattern

**COLOR-STRUCK
STOCKINGS**
page 96
enlarge 500%
cut 2, reverse one

index

159

index *continued*

CREDITS & SOURCES

PHOTO STYLING
*Crafts and decorating – Sue Banker
and Catherine Brett
Food – Catherine Brett and
Carrie Holcomb*

PHOTOGRAHY
*Jason Wilde, Marty Baldwin, Scott
Little, Jason Donnelly, Blaine Moats*

FOOD STYLIST
Dianna Nolan

DESIGNS
*Sue Banker – Cover and pages 8,
11–13, 15, 30–34, 36–37, 42
bottom, 43 top left, 48, 49 bottom,
50 bottom, 56 top and bottom
right, 57 bottom, 69, 73–81, 83,
95, 97, 110, 133–139, 141 bottom,
142–144, 149, and 152.*

Catherine Brett – Page 69.

*Margaret Sindelar – Pages 9–10, 35,
42 top, 43 top right and bottom, 82,
128–129, 131, and 140.*

*Rachel Sindelar – Pages 11, 50 top,
51 bottom, 57 top right, 92–94, 96,
108–109, and 150–151.*

*Alice Wetzel – 12–14, 22–23, 26, 28,
40, 49 top, 51 top, 56 bottom left,
57 top left, 72, 130, 145 top right,
and 153.*

Emma Wetzel – Page 148.

SOURCES
*Page 9 – Leaf table runner fibers
by Weeks Dye Works, 1510-103
Mechanical Blvd., Garner, NC 27529,
www.weeksdyeworks.com; felting
needle tool by Clover Needlecraft
Inc., 13438 Alondra Blvd., Cerritos,
CA 90703-2315, www.clover-usa.
com; buttons by JHB International,
Inc., 1955 S Quince St., Denver, CO
80231–3206, www.buttons.com.*

*Page 82 – Snowflake throw beads by
The Beadery, PO Box 178,
Hope Valley, RI 02832,
www.thebeadery.com; felting tool
by Clover Needlecraft, Inc., 13438
Alondra Blvd., Cerritos, CA 90703-
2315, www.clover-usa.com.*

*Page 140 – Floral tote felt by
National Nonwovens, PO Box 150,
Easthampton, MA 01027,
800/333-3469; beads by The
Beadery, PO Box 178, Hope Valley,
RI 02832, www.thebeadery.com;
felting tool by Clover Needlecraft,
Inc., 13438 Alondra Blvd., Cerritos,
CA 90703–2315, www.clover-usa.
com.*